Mifflin
Harcourt

Language Arts
Grade 6

Printed in the U.S.A.

ISBN 978-0-544-26789-3

  4 5 6 7 8 9 10   0982   22 21 20 19 18 17 16

4500589077   B C D E F G

Core Skills Language Arts
GRADE 6
Table of Contents

Table of Contents
Core Skills Language Arts, Grade 6

Introduction

Core Skills Language Arts was developed to help your student improve the language skills he or she needs to succeed. The book emphasizes skills in the key areas of

- grammar
- punctuation
- vocabulary
- writing
- research

About the Book

The book is divided into six units:

- Parts of Speech
- Sentences
- Mechanics
- Vocabulary and Usage
- Writing
- Research Skills

Your student can work through each unit of the book, or you can pinpoint areas for extra practice.

Lessons have specific instructions and examples and are designed for your student to complete independently. Grammar lessons range from using nouns and verbs to constructing better sentences. Writing exercises range from the how-to paragraph to the persuasive essay. With this practice, your student will gain extra confidence as he or she works on daily school lessons or standardized tests.

A thorough answer key is also provided to check the quality of answers.

A Step Toward Success

Practice may not always make perfect, but it is certainly a step in the right direction. The activities in *Core Skills Language Arts* are an excellent way to ensure greater success for your student.

Nouns

A **noun** is a word that names a person, place, thing, or idea.

Examples: boy   Juan   river   Texas   house   beach   joy

List the nouns from the sentences. Label each noun *person*, *place*, *thing*, or *idea*.

1. Carlos spent a week visiting his aunt and uncle.

   _____

2. Their daughter, Mary, is his favorite cousin.

   _____

3. The two children had long discussions about happiness.

   _____

4. The family lives on a ranch in Montana.

   _____

5. On Saturday, my neighbor cooked a delicious meal.

   _____

6. Grandma helped clear the dishes from the table.

   _____

7. Sam did not leave the kitchen until the dishes were clean.

   _____

8. This month we will honor the memory of veterans of our town.

   _____

9. Volunteers will paint a mural at our school.

   _____

10. Dr. García, the mayor, will lead a parade with marching bands.

    _____

11. The lifeguard works two days a week.

    _____

Think about your favorite holiday. Complete the chart below with nouns that explain more about your favorite holiday.

NOUNS

PERSON	
PLACE	
THING	
IDEA	

Write a noun to complete each sentence.

1. Many board games come with _____.

2. The amusement park nearest my home is called _____.

3. I would like to win a _____ in a contest.

4. The game of _____ relies on luck and skill.

5. It takes a lot of _____ to win most games.

Underline each noun.

6. Anne Frank and her parents hid from the Nazis.

7. Friends smuggled food and supplies to them.

8. For two years, the family hid in an attic in Amsterdam.

9. Anne wrote about it in a diary.

10. Her story was made into a movie about love and courage.

11. Pour orange juice into a bowl.

12. Add ice cream to the recipe.

13. Stir the mixture with a spoon.

14. The punch should look like soapy dishwater.

15. Surprise your friends by serving them this delicious beverage.

Common Nouns and Proper Nouns

There are two main types of nouns: **common nouns** and **proper nouns**.

A **common noun** names any person, place, thing, or idea.
Examples: pilot   city   park

A **proper noun** names a particular person, place, or thing. A proper noun begins with a capital letter.
Examples: Amelia Earhart   Chicago   Katmai National Park

Rewrite the sentences correctly. Capitalize each proper noun and underline each common noun.

1. Harriet tubman was born as a slave in the state of maryland.

   _____

2. Her husband, john tubman, was free.

   _____

3. Harriet fled from the plantation of her master.

   _____

4. The former slave found freedom in philadelphia.

   _____

5. Her family and friends were still enslaved.

   _____

6. This courageous woman returned for her sister, mary ann.

   _____

7. Her brother, james, escaped later with his family.

   _____

8. During her life, harriet led many other escapes.

   _____

9. After the civil war, harriet lived in the city of auburn, new york.

   _____

Underline each common noun.

1. Monet was the first painter of the school of painting called Impressionism.

2. The name of this new style came from a painting by Monet called *Impression: Sunrise.*

3. The movement began in nineteenth-century France.

4. Monet was joined by thirty-nine other artists.

5. Those painters included Pierre-Auguste Renoir, Edgar Degas, and Paul Cézanne.

6. The first exhibit of paintings by this group was in Paris in April 1874.

7. The Impressionists wanted to capture on canvas how the eye saw light.

8. These painters were concerned with the way objects reflect light.

9. Monet often painted from a boat on the Seine River.

10. The painter died on December 5, 1926.

11. Children around the world play hopscotch.

12. There are many versions of the game.

13. In my town, Plainview, New York, children draw a board with eight squares.

14. They throw a stone or coin into a square, hop on one foot into each square, and then return.

15. Can you write a paragraph about a sport that you like to play?

Underline each proper noun.

16. Diego Rivera was one of the greatest painters and muralists of Mexico.

17. Because he loved Mexico, his works often portray the culture and history of that country.

18. One of his paintings reflects the time before the Spanish conquered Mexico.

19. That painting shows the Zapotec Indians making gold jewelry.

20. Although Rivera did some of his most famous murals in Mexico City, several of his works were painted in the United States.

21. Visit the Detroit Institute of Arts in Michigan to see some of the best works by Diego Rivera.

22. The Constitution of the United States was drafted at the Constitutional Convention.

23. Leaders from around the country met in Philadelphia, Pennsylvania.

24. The Bill of Rights was written by James Madison.

25. On April 30, 1789, George Washington took office as the leader of the country.

Read the following sentences. Draw one line under each common noun. Circle each proper noun.

The four generals met beside the river. General Tang raised his violin and began playing a sad tune.

"Oh, I cannot bear to feel such sorrow," said General Wang. So Tang played a bright, happy song.

"How wonderful!" exclaimed General Lang. "That melody fills me with joy!"

"Yes," agreed General Mang. "But we have not come to this place to hear songs. We have come to discuss the future of our country. How can we be certain that this peace will last?"

Write common or proper nouns to complete the webs below. Use nouns from the paragraphs above. Then add two more nouns to each web.

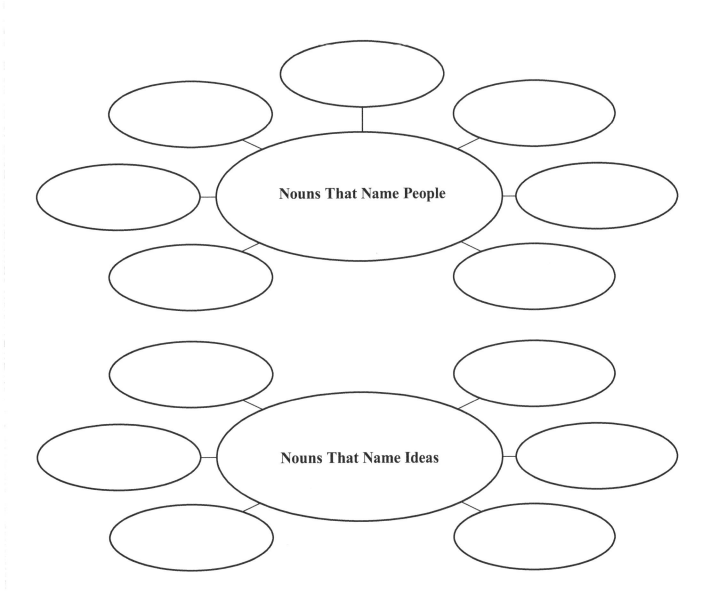

5

Singular and Plural Nouns

A **singular noun** names one person, place, or thing.

Examples: principal   cafeteria   stereo

A **plural noun** names more than one person, place, or thing.

Examples: principals   cafeterias   stereos

Add *s* to most nouns to make them plural.

Examples: principal, principals   building, buildings

Add *es* to most nouns ending in *ch*, *sh*, *s*, or *x* to make them plural.

Examples: switch, switches   wish, wishes   box, boxes

If a noun ends in a consonant and *y*, change the *y* to *i* and add *es*.

Examples: community, communities   party, parties

If a noun ends in a vowel and *y*, add *s* to make it plural.

Examples: toy, toys   play, plays

Complete each sentence by writing the plural form of the noun in ( ).

1. Sally's family has _____.
   (horse)

2. They have _____, too.
   (donkey)

3. Sally's favorite horse is white with _____ of brown.
   (patch)

4. She always goes riding on clear _____.
   (day)

5. Her _____ like to trot along behind the horse.
   (puppy)

6. She waves to neighbors on their _____.
   (porch)

7. Several _____ like to ride with her.
   (lady)

8. They never wear _____ for riding.
   (dress)

9. Sally likes to ride over the _____.
   (hill)

10. She gallops through the _____.
    (pass)

Some nouns ending in *f* or *fe* are made plural by changing the *f* or *fe* to **ves**.

Examples: leaf, leaves   wife, wives

Some nouns ending in *f* are made plural by adding *s*.

Examples: roof, roofs   chief, chiefs

Most nouns ending in *o* that have a vowel just before the *o* are made plural by adding *s*.

Examples: radio, radios   stereo, stereos

Some nouns ending in *o* preceded by a consonant are made plural by adding *es*, but others are made plural by adding only *s*.

Examples: potato, potatoes   piano, pianos

A few nouns have irregular plural forms.

Examples: foot, feet   mouse, mice

A few nouns have the same form for both the singular and plural.

Examples: sheep, sheep   trout, trout

Complete each sentence by writing the plural form of the noun in ( ).

1. Two _____ live on a farm in Alaska.
   (woman)

2. The farmers take many _____ of the animals.
   (photo)

3. The _____ on the farm have had _____.
   (ox)   (calf)

4. The farmers also raise _____.
   (sheep)

5. _____ sometimes try to attack them.
   (Wolf)

6. A wolf's _____ are as sharp as _____.
   (tooth)   (knife)

7. Some of the land is used to grow _____.
   (potato)

8. The farmers grow _____ during the summer.
   (tomato)

9. _____ eat the _____ of the plants.
   (Deer)   (leaf)

10. _____ often wander through the farm.
    (Moose)

11. _____ swim in the streams nearby.
    (Trout)

12. One woman has two _____.
    (child)

Write the plural form for each singular noun and the singular form for each plural noun.

1. brush
_____

2. lice
_____

3. butterflies
_____

4. man
_____

5. suitcases
_____

6. turkey
_____

7. watches
_____

8. melody
_____

9. cheeses
_____

10. gases
_____

11. cranberry
_____

12. scarf
_____

13. hero
_____

14. ax
_____

15. blueberries
_____

16. geese
_____

17. mouth
_____

18. reef
_____

19. canary
_____

20. glitches
_____

21. umbrellas
_____

22. wells
_____

23. vase
_____

24. mosses
_____

25. lance
_____

26. mass
_____

27. patch
_____

28. video
_____

29. baby
_____

30. gulch
_____

31. cello
_____

32. sash
_____

Name _____ Date _____

Possessive Nouns

A **possessive noun** shows ownership or possession.

A **singular possessive noun** shows ownership by one person or thing. To form the possessive of most singular nouns, add an apostrophe (') and *s*.

Examples: my aunt's house   the tree's limbs

A **plural possessive noun** shows ownership by more than one person or thing. To form the possessive of a plural noun that ends in *s*, add an apostrophe (').

Examples: my friends' parents   the teachers' classes

To form the possessive of a plural noun that does not end in *s*, add an apostrophe (') and *s*.

Examples: the men's shoes   the mice's cheese

Rewrite each phrase using a possessive noun.

1. the book by Lewis Carroll _____

2. the edge of the knife _____

3. the cover of the book _____

4. the speech given by Mayor Sanita _____

5. the aroma of the flowers _____

6. the bicycle that belongs to the children _____

7. the roar of the sirens _____

8. the colors of the rainbow _____

9. the shoes that Chris owns _____

10. the purses that belong to the women _____

Write a possessive noun to complete each sentence.

11. I saw the _____ smile.

12. The _____ spots will not come off.

13. My _____ stories always make me laugh.

14. At midnight, you can see the _____ glow.

15. _____ illustrations are amazing.

Name _____ Date _____

Write the singular possessive form of each noun.

1. sculptor _____

2. artist _____

3. hour _____

4. country _____

5. thief _____

6. Robert Frost _____

7. week _____

8. minute _____

9. weaver _____

10. Samuel Clemens _____

11. wolf _____

12. nurse _____

13. King Henry _____

14. moment _____

15. secretary _____

16. Mr. Jones _____

Write the plural possessive form of each noun.

17. hostesses _____

18. teachers _____

19. women _____

20. masters _____

21. workers _____

22. hours _____

23. oxen _____

24. spies _____

25. buffaloes _____

26. surgeons _____

27. sheep _____

28. secretaries _____

Rewrite each sentence. Use a possessive noun in the underlined phrase.

29. Charles Green was <u>the worst balloonist in Britain</u>.

_____

30. With <u>the help of a colleague</u>, he prepared for flight.

_____

31. Suddenly, <u>the ropes of the balloon</u> slipped off.

_____

32. How surprised the onlookers must have been to hear <u>the calls for help from the flyers</u>!

_____

Write the possessive form of each noun in parentheses. Then label the possessive noun *singular* or *plural*.

1. (Luis) family celebrated Christmas together.

   _____

2. The (children) grandmother had the celebration at her ranch.

   _____

3. Their (parents) car was loaded with gifts.

   _____

4. They drove past the (sheep) pens on the way to the house.

   _____

5. They saw that the lettuce had become two (deer) dinner.

   _____

6. They could see their (cousins) faces through the window.

   _____

7. Each (person) gift from Grandmother was a sweater.

   _____

8. The (adults) sweaters were larger than the (children).

   _____

9. A turkey from the (Wilsons) ranch was the main course.

   _____

10. (Uncle Bernie) stuffing was a success as usual.

    _____

11. That night, we went to the (neighbor) house to sing Christmas carols.

    _____

12. This was our (families) best Christmas ever!

    _____

13. The (boys) clothing department is over here.

    _____

14. The (baby) car seat is in the truck.

    _____

Pronouns

A **pronoun** takes the place of one or more than one noun.

Examples: I   you   he   she   it   we
          they   me   him   her   us   them

Write the pronoun from each sentence. Then write the noun that each pronoun refers to.

1. Some stories are designed to teach lessons; they are called fables.

   _____

2. Aesop, a Greek slave, died more than two thousand years ago, but he is still famous.

   _____

3. Aesop told stories because he wanted to teach lessons.

   _____

4. A story about a discontented donkey was first told by Aesop; it is one of Aesop's best fables.

   _____

5. This fable is about a donkey and how it wanted to be treated better.

   _____

6. The donkey's owner had a dog she treated well.

   _____

Rewrite each sentence, replacing appropriate nouns with pronouns.

7. The owner gave the dog a soft bed and fed the dog well.

   _____

8. The donkey tried to make its owner treat the donkey well.

   _____

9. The donkey learned that the donkey should not try to be somebody else.

   _____

10. Can you write two fables and illustrate the fables?

   _____

Agreement of Pronouns with Antecedents

When using a pronoun, make sure its **antecedent**, the noun to which it refers, is clear.

Example: *Nicolás* heard.   *He* heard.

Pronouns should agree with their antecedents in **number** and **gender**. Number tells whether a pronoun is singular or plural. Gender tells whether a pronoun is masculine, feminine, or neuter.

Example: *Nicolás* heard *a librarian* tell *stories*.   *He* heard *her* tell *them*.

In the above example, *He* is singular and masculine, *her* is singular and feminine, and *them* is plural and neuter.

Underline the pronoun in each sentence. Circle the antecedent. If the pronoun and antecedent don't agree, rewrite the sentence using the correct pronoun.

1. Thurgood Marshall was born in Maryland; his grandfather had been taken to Maryland as a slave.

   _____

2. Marshall's parents wanted to give her son a good education.

   _____

3. Marshall's mother was a teacher in the school her son attended.

   _____

4. Marshall decided it wanted to be a lawyer.

   _____

5. Marshall attended Howard University Law School. She accepted black students when many other schools did not.

   _____

Write the pronoun in parentheses that correctly completes each sentence.

6. Marshall's mother sold _____ engagement ring to help pay for law school.
   (his, her)

7. Marshall was grateful to _____.
   (him, her)

8. Marshall later graduated first in _____ class.
   (his, their)

9. President Johnson appointed _____ to the Supreme Court.
   (him, them)

10. When people disagree with a court decision, _____ appeal to the Supreme Court.
   (they, it)

Vague Pronouns

When you use a pronoun, be sure that its antecedent is clear.

Example: Joey told his dad that *his* soup was getting cold.

Whose soup was getting cold—Joey's or his dad's? Rewriting the sentence makes the meaning clear.

Examples: Joey said, "Dad, *your* soup is getting cold." **or** Joey said, "Dad, *my* soup is getting cold."

Underline the pronoun or pronouns in each sentence. Circle the nouns to which the pronoun might refer. Rewrite the sentence so that its meaning is clear.

1. Maribel likes math, science, and gym, but it is her favorite.

   _____

2. Patrick told his uncle that he needed to leave for the game soon.

   _____

3. Although I enjoy watching both baseball and soccer, I don't understand how to play it.

   _____

4. My brother dropped a plate on his foot and broke it.

   _____

5. Anna told Lucy she needed to visit her aunt to learn how to play tennis.

   _____

6. After Rodrigo missed his brother's band concert, he felt sad.

   _____

7. My dog laid his bone on the old rug and then began to chew on it.

   _____

8. My sister bought an old bicycle with a new paint job, but it was in poor condition.

   _____

Subject and Object Pronouns

A **subject pronoun** is used as the subject or as part of the subject of a sentence. The subject pronouns are *I, you, he, she, it, we,* and *they.*

Example: *We* are ready to go.

An **object pronoun** is used as a direct or indirect object in a sentence. It can also be used after a preposition. The object pronouns are *me, you, him, her, it, us,* and *them.*

Example: Rebecca gave *me* a gift.   Rebecca gave the gift to *him.*

Complete each sentence by circling the correct pronoun in parentheses. Then write *subject pronoun* **or** *object pronoun* **to identify the form you used.**

1. Aunt Alicia gave (we, us) a book about Elizabeth Blackwell.

   _____

2. Elizabeth Blackwell's life story was fascinating to Lisa and (I, me).

   _____

3. (She, Her) and her sister became doctors.

   _____

4. (She, Her) was the first woman in the United States to enter medical school.

   _____

5. Other people disapproved of (she, her).

   _____

6. According to Daniel, (we, us) have many more opportunities than the girls in Blackwell's day.

   _____

7. (He, Him) and his brother will have the same opportunities that women have.

   _____

8. Women like Elizabeth Blackwell have helped (we, us) by their example.

   _____

9. I admire (she, her) and her sister.

   _____

10. My father always tells (I, me) that I can become anything I want to be if I work hard.

    _____

11. I believe (he, him).

    _____

12. Can (you, him) reach for the stars?

    _____

13. Patricia and (I, me) will sing for you.

    _____

14. (They, Them) are ready to play soccer.

    _____

15. Bring (he, him) some paper and a pencil.

    _____

Write the pronoun in parentheses that correctly completes each sentence.

1. My friends and _____ wish Anna Pavlova were still alive and dancing.
   (I, me)

2. _____ ballet fans consider her one of the greatest dancers of all time.
   (We, Us)

3. Anna's parents took _____ to a ballet.
   (she, her)

4. _____ encouraged their daughter to dance.
   (They, Them)

5. Anna later made _____ very proud.
   (they, them)

6. Anna met the great dancer Vaslav Nijinsky and danced with _____.
   (he, him)

7. I am sure _____ made a wonderful dancing couple.
   (they, them)

8. I wish I could have seen _____ dance.
   (they, them)

9. Perhaps _____ too will become a great dancer someday.
   (I, me)

10. _____ had a strange experience.
    (We, Us)

11. How did _____ get here?
    (I, me)

12. _____ were staring at the television.
    (They, Them)

13. Tell _____ what that is.
    (he, him)

14. People sang and danced for _____ all the time.
    (she, her)

15. Everyone was staring at _____.
    (they, them)

Find two pronouns you did not use in the exercise above. Use each pronoun in a sentence.

_____

_____

_____

_____

_____

Possessive Pronouns

A **possessive pronoun** shows ownership or possession of something.

The possessive pronouns *my, your, his, her, its, our,* and *their* are used before nouns.
Example: Jerome is learning about *his* ancestors.

The possessive pronouns *mine, yours, his, hers, ours,* and *theirs* stand alone.
Examples: The picture is *his.*   The books are *mine.*

Rewrite each sentence. Use possessive pronouns to make the sentence less wordy.

1. Annie Oakley was famous for the shooting ability of Annie Oakley.

   _____

2. Mr. Oakley let her use the gun that he owned.

   _____

3. Buffalo Bill made Annie a star in the show that he had.

   _____

4. Annie never missed the target for which she aimed.

   _____

5. Audiences could hardly believe the eyes that belonged to them.

   _____

6. Jeremy wants to use the stereo that belongs to you.

   _____

7. The dog devoured the food that he had.

   _____

8. The Reynas had the couch that they owned reupholstered.

   _____

9. I want to change the schedule that belongs to me.

   _____

Name _____ Date _____

Complete each sentence with a possessive pronoun.

1. Residents of St. Petersburg, Russia, are proud of _____ city.

2. We traveled to St. Petersburg to visit _____ friends.

3. Boris took us to see some of the most beautiful sights in _____ native city.

4. Marie and I, together with _____ friends, took a boat down the canals of the city.

5. Boris pointed out palaces where some of Russia's great rulers had made _____ homes.

6. At night, the sun still shed _____ light on the city.

7. On nights at home, Russians love to make tea; it is _____ favorite beverage.

8. Tea and apple cake is a favorite late-night snack of _____.

9. St. Petersburg is full of flea markets where merchants show off _____ wares.

10. The traders set up _____ stalls along Nevsky Prospekt.

11. Marie invited us on a trip to one of _____ favorite places, the Kirov Islands.

12. This place has a charm all _____ own.

13. During World War II, the citizens of St. Petersburg endured a 900-day siege of _____ city by the Germans.

14. We saw a man with a ribbon on _____ coat, showing that he was a veteran of that siege.

15. People who suffered through that period wear _____ ribbons proudly.

16. Snow, ice, hunger, and disease took _____ toll among the brave residents of St. Petersburg.

17. _____ name at the time was Leningrad, in honor of Lenin, a leader of the revolution of 1917.

Reflexive Pronouns

> A **reflexive pronoun** usually refers to the subject of a sentence.
>
> The reflexive pronouns are *myself, yourself, himself, herself, itself, ourselves, yourselves,* and *themselves.*
>
> *Example:*   Marie found *herself* alone in the quiet forest.
>
> An **intensive pronoun** adds emphasis by referring back to a noun or pronoun.
>
> *Example:*   *I* cooked that lasagna *myself.*

Underline each reflexive or intensive pronoun. Write the word to which it refers.

1. Diane shook the sand off herself.

   _____

2. We went to hear the author himself speak.

   _____

3. The members of the other team warmed themselves up by swimming laps.

   _____

4. We discussed the race among ourselves.

   _____

5. I myself would not have agreed to wake up at 5 a.m.

   _____

6. Did Joe himself bake that apple pie?

   _____

7. The dog dried itself off by rolling in the grass.

   _____

8. Ed and Beverly made themselves a mushroom and sausage pizza.

   _____

9. I chopped the bell peppers and the onions myself.

   _____

10. Estella and I won a prize for ourselves.

    _____

Complete each sentence with a reflexive or intensive pronoun that agrees with its antecedent.

11. Elaine's towel was not in the pile when she went to dry _____.

12. The beach _____ was covered with fine white sand.

13. The picnic basket was packed by Ben _____.

14. Be sure you dry _____ well.

15. We must protect _____ from the cold.

16. The swimmers _____ dress very quickly.

Indefinite Pronouns

An **indefinite pronoun** is a pronoun that does not refer to a specific person, place, thing, or idea.

Some indefinite pronouns are *everyone, everything, everybody, anybody, many, most, few, each, some, someone, all, nothing, nobody,* and *no one.*

Example: *Someone* is knocking at the door.

An indefinite pronoun can be singular or plural. Follow the rules for subject-verb agreement when using indefinite pronouns as subjects.

Examples: *Some* of the girls are absent. *Everyone* is sick.

Write the indefinite pronoun from each sentence. Then write *singular* or *plural* to identify the indefinite pronoun.

1. Everyone seems to be leaving. _____

2. Some have to stay. _____

3. Everything needs to be picked up. _____

4. Is anybody volunteering? _____

5. I see that many of you want to leave. _____

Write the verb form in parentheses that correctly completes each sentence.

6. Most of you _____ been fairly neat.
   (has, have)

7. A few _____ problems for the rest.
   (creates, create)

8. If each of you _____, it will not take long to clean up the mess.
   (helps, help)

9. Someone _____ to carry the trash to the bins.
   (needs, need)

10. All of us _____ to go home.
    (want, wants)

11. Now nothing _____ out of place.
    (is, are)

Who, Whom, Whose

Use **who** as a subject pronoun and **whom** as an object pronoun.

Examples: *Who* is not going?   To *whom* am I speaking?

Do not confuse the possessive pronoun *whose* with the contraction *who's*.

Examples: *Whose* books are these?   *Who's* that at the door?

Write *who* or *whom* to complete each sentence.

1. _____ will help decorate the gym for the costume party?

2. _____ did you call?

3. Do you know _____ is planning to attend?

4. With _____ are you going?

5. _____ are you going to pretend to be?

6. From _____ did you get that idea?

7. Do you think the others will know _____ you are?

8. _____ can pick up the refreshments?

9. From _____ do we get the money to pay for them?

10. _____ is going to be the costume judge?

Write *whose* or *who's* to complete each sentence.

11. _____ going to drive everyone?

12. _____ parents have a van?

13. _____ your favorite cartoon character?

14. _____ the boy in the Napoleon costume?

15. This mask is mine, but _____ mask is that?

16. _____ costume did you borrow?

17. _____ Bradley supposed to be?

18. _____ selecting the best costume?

Using Pronouns

Underline the pronouns in each sentence.

1. Leon asked Anne to tell him about some of her favorite books.

2. "Okay," Anne told him.

3. She chose two books and opened them.

4. Here are a few of the biographies about women pioneers.

5. I could talk about one of them.

6. Leon told her to pick one.

7. He enjoyed it.

8. I have been reading about Marie Dorion.

9. When Marie accompanied the trappers to Oregon, they showed her great respect.

10. Marie loved Pierre Dorion and traveled with him.

11. One day, Marie found herself alone in the quiet forest.

12. Marie Dorion untied the horse and loaded it with supplies.

13. As the three of them left, Marie Dorion made herself a promise—that she and her children would survive.

14. Nine days later, a snowstorm trapped her and the boys.

15. The Dorions kept themselves alive for 53 days.

16. The Wallawalla Indians found Marie Dorion; they rescued her and the boys.

17. Anna Taylor went to Niagara Falls, but she crossed it differently.

18. Witnesses watched with their mouths open.

19. Taylor squeezed herself into a barrel.

20. Was she the first person to survive a trip over Niagara Falls?

21. The Kung people use eggshells to store their water supply.

22. A Ndaka bride is carried to her wedding on a shaded platform; indeed, the day is almost entirely hers.

23. Monica told herself that she must drive slowly.

24. Monica's younger sister and brother were with her.

25. Bob said that he was hungry.

26. The children amused themselves by singing.

27. Cars pulled off the highway because it was icy.

28. Monica drove slowly, but she still lost control.

29. For a moment, she found herself helpless.

30. Then she maneuvered the car and stopped it.

31. Marla and Darnell both told me the news, but I didn't believe them at first.

32. I asked Mr. O'Reilly, but he hadn't heard anything about it.

33. Then Trina ran in and said that she had seen the whole thing.

34. After Trina explained just what had happened, I thanked her as politely as I could.

35. Then I smiled secretly, just to myself, and hurried away.

Adjectives

An **adjective** is a word that modifies, or describes, a noun or a pronoun.

Example: We saw *lazy* lions beneath a *shady* tree.

Adjectives tell *what kind, how many,* or *which one.*

Examples: *lazy* lions, *three* adults, *that* tree

The adjectives *a, an,* and *the* are called **articles**.

Use *a* before a word that begins with a consonant sound.

Examples: *a* lion, *a* tree

Use *an* before a word that begins with a vowel sound.

Examples: *an* adventure, *an* older lioness

Write each adjective. Label it *article* or *describing*.

1. Russia is an enormous country.

   _____

2. It has long, cold winters.

   _____

3. Rich crops are grown in the black, fertile earth.

   _____

4. Many of the farms have early harvests.

   _____

5. The lion is a sociable creature.

   _____

6. A lioness, calm but alert, watches over the smallest cub.

   _____

7. Cubs learn important skills at an early age.

   _____

8. Nightly hunts may provide rich feasts.

   _____

Change the meaning and tone of each sentence by replacing the adjectives. Write each new sentence.

1. The empty countryside has a lonely feeling.

   _____

2. We had a dull, boring visit in the dreary forests of Russia.

   _____

3. We then returned to the lively, bustling cities of the United States.

   _____

Use adjectives and articles to complete these sentences.

4. When the _____ lion is on the prowl, other _____
   animals must be cautious.

5. _____ wildebeest or _____ antelope could become a

   _____ lion's dinner.

6. Then the pride of lions, _____, and _____ might settle

   in for a _____ nap.

Imagine that you are an archaeologist being interviewed about the ancient Egyptians and their way of life. Use adjectives to answer the reporter's questions.

7. What words describe their kingdoms?

   _____

8. What type of person do you think a king or queen had to be in ancient Egypt?

   _____

9. What words describe their clothing and jewelry?

   _____

10. How do you feel about your most recent discovery?

    _____

Proper Adjectives

A **proper adjective** is an adjective that is formed from a proper noun. A proper adjective always begins with a capital letter.

Examples:

Proper Noun	Proper Adjective
Africa	African
Scotland	Scottish

Write the proper adjective from each sentence. Then write the proper noun from which the proper adjective was formed.

1. The African nations were especially interesting.

    _____

2. We bought some beautiful Hungarian crystal.

    _____

3. The English language was spoken there.

    _____

4. Our German friend came with us on our trip around the world.

    _____

5. Joyce enjoyed the Italian paintings.

    _____

6. Ralph liked the visit to a Tibetan monastery.

    _____

7. I studied Islamic law at the university.

    _____

8. Ron purchased a postcard with a picture of Nefertiti, a beautiful Egyptian queen.

    _____

9. We purchased Japanese paper for origami.

    _____

10. The Mexican pottery was less expensive at the market.

    _____

Write a sentence using the proper adjective formed from each proper noun.

11. China (Chinese) _____

12. Spain (Spanish) _____

13. Armenia (Armenian) _____

14. Britain (British) _____

15. Texas (Texan) _____

Name _____ Date _____

This, That, These, Those

> A **demonstrative adjective** tells which one. The words *this, that, these,* and *those* are demonstrative adjectives.
>
> *Example:*   *This* book has more illustrations than *those* magazines.

Write the demonstrative adjective from each sentence. Label the demonstrative adjective *singular* or *plural*.

1. This open house is going to be a real success.

   _____

2. Ask those students to come and help.

   _____

3. These science projects need to be arranged.

   _____

4. Where shall we display these drawings?

   _____

5. Put them on that bulletin board.

   _____

6. You must seize this opportunity.

   _____

Label each underlined word *adjective* or *pronoun*. Rewrite each sentence in which *this, that, these,* or *those* is used as a pronoun. Change the pronoun to a demonstrative adjective.

7. What shall I do with <u>these</u>? _____

8. Arrange them on <u>that</u> table. _____

9. Do we have any more of <u>those</u>? _____

10. Look in <u>this</u> drawer. _____

11. Did you draw <u>that</u>? _____

12. Are <u>those</u> maps clear? _____

13. Shall I look in <u>these</u>? _____

14. <u>That</u> table is covered with books and maps. _____

Predicate Adjectives

> A **predicate adjective** is an adjective that follows a linking verb and describes the subject of a sentence. Forms of *be* are the most common linking verbs. Other linking verbs include forms of *taste, look, smell, feel, appear, seem*, and *become*.
>
> *Example:*   I look *tired*, but I feel *fine*.

Write the predicate adjective from each sentence. Then write the word it modifies.

1. The air feels warm today. _____

2. The flowers smell unusually sweet. _____

3. High in the sky is the sun. _____

4. The horses look peaceful in the meadow. _____

5. Sharon feels happy outside. _____

6. She is eager for a ride on her horse. _____

7. Her horse appears ready to go. _____

8. How beautiful is the day! _____

9. The surgeon was skillful in the operating room. _____

10. The mango tastes bitter, but I will eat it anyway. _____

11. That horse at the far end of the meadow is fast. _____

12. Its coat appears gray in the shade. _____

13. However, it becomes silver in the bright sun. _____

14. Horses like that are unusual. _____

15. They are usually well trained. _____

16. Rin Tin Tin and Lassie seem brave in their movies. _____

17. When audiences watched, they felt good. _____

18. Rin Tin Tin looked fearless. _____

Use the linking verb to write a sentence containing a predicate adjective.

19. feel _____

20. taste _____

Comparison with Adjectives: *er, est*

An adjective has three degrees of **comparison: positive, comparative,** and **superlative.**

The **positive degree** of an adjective is used when no comparison is being made.

Example: This is a *hot* day.

The **comparative degree** of an adjective is used to compare two items. Form the comparative of most one-syllable adjectives by adding *er*.

Example: Today is *hotter* than yesterday.

The **superlative degree** of an adjective is used to compare three or more items. Form the superlative of most one-syllable adjectives by adding *est*.

Example: This is the *hottest* day of the year.

Write the comparative form and the superlative form of each adjective.

Positive	Comparative	Superlative
1. cold	_____	_____
2. safe	_____	_____
3. funny	_____	_____
4. flat	_____	_____
5. shiny	_____	_____
6. tall	_____	_____
7. white	_____	_____
8. sweet	_____	_____
9. sad	_____	_____
10. young	_____	_____

Write the form of the adjective in parentheses that correctly completes the sentence.

11. France is _____ than Luxembourg.
         (large)

12. Austria is _____ than France.
         (small)

13. Luxembourg is the _____ of the three countries.
                    (small)

Name _____ Date _____

Other Comparisons

Use *more* or *less* and *most* or *least* to form the comparative and the superlative of most adjectives with two or more syllables.

Examples: wonderful   more wonderful   most wonderful

                wonderful   less wonderful   least wonderful

Some adjectives have special forms for comparing. Memorize adjectives that change spelling completely in the comparative and the superlative degrees.

Examples: good   better   best

Write the comparative form and the superlative form of each adjective.

Positive	Comparative	Superlative
1. energetic		
2. difficult		
3. generous		
4. affectionate		
5. active		
6. bad		
7. much		
8. likely		
9. expensive		
10. crowded		

Rewrite each sentence. Use the form of the adjective in parentheses that correctly completes the sentence.

11. Ruffles is the (beautiful) puppy of the litter.

_____

12. Sport is (intelligent) than Ruffles.

_____

13. Of all the puppies, Tuffy is the (playful).

_____

Using Adjectives

Write the correct degree of comparison for the adjective in parentheses.

1. The stone houses of wealthy Mayas looked _____ (strong) and

   _____ (impressive) than those of their poorer neighbors.

2. The clothing of Mayan priests was the _____ (elaborate) of all.

3. The _____ (beautiful) city of Tenochtitlán may have been the

   Aztecs' _____ (great) achievement.

4. The Incas, who seem to have been _____ (aggressive) than

   the Aztecs or Mayas, ruled the _____ (large) empire in the hemisphere.

5. We were all competing to see who could create the _____ (good) poster
   about an ancient civilization.

6. The Great Wall of China wasn't a _____ (bad) idea at all!

7. This poster is definitely _____ (good) than last year's winner.

8. Ms. Mata is feeling _____ (good) than she did yesterday, rather than

   _____ (bad), so she'll judge the posters this afternoon.

9. This contest has been _____ (enjoyable) than last year's contest.

10. In fact, it may be the _____ (good) activity of the year.

Underline the adjectives in each sentence below.

11. The fierce battle at Gettysburg took place in 1863.

12. This battle was not the first conflict of the Civil War.

13. Few Southerners reached Union lines.

14. A general named Robert E. Lee led the Confederate army.

15. The Confederates approached under heavy gunfire.

16. That army would not turn back during an attack.

17. Many soldiers on both sides were killed.

18. Gettysburg is a pivotal battle in the Civil War.

19. President Lincoln visited the site several months later.

20. He read a memorable speech, now known as the Gettysburg Address.

Action Verbs

An **action verb** tells what the subject of a sentence does or did.

Examples: She *sleeps* every day. She *slept* yesterday.

Underline the action verb in each sentence.

1. Dr. James Naismith originated the game of basketball.

2. The Hillside team and the Seaside team compete every year.

3. The two centers leaped for the ball.

4. They stretched their arms high into the air.

5. A Hillside forward grabbed the ball.

6. The forward dribbled the ball to the end of the court.

7. She aimed for the basket.

8. The ball flew through the air.

9. The ball bounced off the backboard.

10. Several players jumped for the ball.

Rewrite each sentence. Use a strong action verb to make the sentence more vivid.

11. A Seaside forward got the ball.

_____

12. Her teammate went to the other end of the court.

_____

13. The forward sent the ball the length of the court.

_____

14. Romelia put the ball into the basket.

_____

15. The Seaside fans and players yelled excitedly.

_____

Linking Verbs

A **linking verb** connects the subject of a sentence to a noun that renames the subject or to an adjective that describes it.

The most common linking verb is *be*. Some forms of *be* are *am*, *is*, *are*, *was*, and *were*.

Example: Carolyn *is* tired.

Write the verb from each sentence. Label it *action* or *linking*.

1. The family celebrated Thanksgiving at Uncle Tomás's house.

   _____

2. His house is large enough for us all.

   _____

3. His table reaches from one end of the dining room to the other.

   _____

4. Uncle Tomás cooked the whole dinner by himself.

   _____

5. He appeared tired.

   _____

6. However, he greeted everyone with warmth and enthusiasm.

   _____

7. The turkey smelled wonderful.

   _____

8. Everyone became impatient.

   _____

9. The dinner table looked beautiful.

   _____

10. The greenhouse effect is a danger to our environment.

    _____

11. Heat rises.

    _____

12. Some heat energy escapes Earth's atmosphere.

    _____

13. Many gases are colorless and odorless.

    _____

14. High levels of carbon dioxide were present.

    _____

15. The Industrial Revolution was a turning point for the environment.

    _____

16. Many researchers study global warming.

    _____

17. Our community recycles glass, newspaper, and aluminum.

    _____

18. It was a terrific place.

    _____

19. Connie opened the big umbrella.

    _____

20. The king and queen were quite argumentative.

    _____

Name _____ Date _____

Action Verbs and Linking Verbs

Read the following passage. Then underline the action verbs and circle the linking verbs.

Marathoners are amazing athletes. They compete in races more than 26 miles long. The best marathoners are usually small and slight. They need very strong legs and powerful lungs, too. Youth, however, is not necessarily an advantage in a marathon.

This long race carries the name of an ancient battlefield. In 490 B.C., the Greeks defeated the Persians at Marathon. According to legend, a Greek soldier ran all the way from Marathon to Athens with news of the victory. He ran more than 20 miles. Now a marathon is a regular part of the Olympic Games. The official distance for an Olympic marathon is 42,195 meters, or 26 miles and 385 yards.

Complete the following sentences. Add the kind of verb identified in parentheses.

1. The team members _____ every day.
                      (action)

2. Their coach _____ them.
            (action)

3. The day of the big race _____.
                  (action)

4. The athletes _____ enthusiastic.
             (linking)

5. They _____.
       (action)

6. Coal, oil, and natural gas _____ fossil fuels.
                  (linking)

7. Dr. Huong _____ global warning.
            (action)

8. Some students _____ a model of our planet.
              (action)

9. Wood _____ a renewable resource.
        (linking)

10. Technology _____ problems as well as solutions.
            (action)

Main Verbs and Helping Verbs

> A **verb phrase** is made up of two or more verbs. The **main verb** is the most important verb in a verb phrase.
>
> *Example:*   My teacher was ___***born***___ in Venezuela.
>
> The last word of a verb phrase is the main verb. The other words are **helping verbs**.
>
> *Example:*   My teacher ___***was***___ born in Venezuela.

Underline the verb phrase and circle the main verb in each sentence.

1. The Powells are moving.

2. They have lived next door for ten years.

3. I am missing them already.

4. Their son has been my best friend for a long time.

5. The family had moved here from California.

6. Why do they want a different house?

7. Mrs. Powell has accepted a job in New York.

8. Her sister is living in New York.

9. She was working for a large publishing company.

10. The same company did offer Mrs. Powell a job.

11. Does she like big cities?

12. She was not complaining in her last letter.

13. She had lived in Chicago at one time.

14. She is enjoying the museums.

15. Mr. Powell will find a good job.

16. Their son has entered school.

17. He might meet many new friends.

18. A tai chi master may visit our school.

19. His daughter is living in the United States.

20. She could give us a lesson in tai chi.

Name _____ Date _____

Write *main verb* or *helping verb* to identify the underlined verb in each sentence.

1. The tiny curtain <u>will</u> slowly open.   _____

2. Two figures <u>are</u> dancing into view.   _____

3. The figures are <u>called</u> puppets.   _____

4. Puppets can be <u>made</u> out of cloth and wood.   _____

5. Our puppet theater may <u>give</u> three shows a year.   _____

6. Each show <u>is</u> performed for four weekends.   _____

7. New plays are <u>rehearsed</u> carefully.   _____

8. I <u>have</u> become a puppeteer with the company.   _____

9. I <u>am</u> memorizing lines and movements.   _____

10. The new play was <u>written</u> in Spanish and English.   _____

11. Sometimes, our lines are <u>spoken</u> in English.   _____

12. Sometimes, audiences <u>have</u> asked for Spanish.   _____

13. All the puppeteers <u>can</u> speak both languages.   _____

14. We <u>should</u> do this for several years.   _____

15. <u>Do</u> the audiences enjoy the shows?   _____

Complete these sentences with the main verbs and helping verbs from the box.

are	were	does	need	should
will	be	blooming	picked	visit

16. The roses _____ _____ today.

17. The garden _____ _____ beautiful next year.

18. Everyone _____ _____ during the summer.

19. A sturdy sunflower _____ not _____ support.

20. The apples _____ already _____.

Principal Parts of Verbs

The **principal parts** of verbs are the **present, present participle, past,** and **past participle.**

For regular verbs, the present participle is formed by adding *ing* to the present. It is used with a form of the helping verb *be.*

The past and past participle of regular verbs are formed by adding *ed* or *d* to the present. The past participle uses a form of the helping verb *have.*

Examples:	**Present**	**Present Participle**	**Past**	**Past Participle**
	play	(is, are, am) playing	played	(have, has, had) played
	move	(is, are, am) moving	moved	(have, has, had) moved

An irregular verb forms its past and past participle in other ways. A dictionary shows the principal parts of these verbs.

Underline the main verb in each sentence. Write *present,* *present participle,* *past,* **or** *past participle* **to label the main verbs.**

1. Randy's class studies world history.   _____

2. The students are reading about the Renaissance.   _____

3. The teacher has taught them about the art of that time.   _____

4. They have learned much about Renaissance painting.   _____

5. Yesterday, they visited an art museum.   _____

6. They had always gone to a different museum before.   _____

7. They had seen a display of Egyptian art at the Egyptian Museum. _____

8. The English teachers had read two new novels.   _____

9. The band director is planning the fall musical.   _____

10. The cafeteria monitor talks to the children.   _____

Write the correct form of the verb in parentheses in each sentence. At the end of each sentence, label the verb *present,* *present participle,* *past,* **or** *past participle.*

11. These days the class _____ something about history every week. (learn)

_____

12. Today the students are _____ a movie about Leonardo da Vinci. (watch)

_____

Name _____ Date _____

Write the present participle, past, and past participle of each verb.

Present	Present Participle (with *is, are, am*)	Past	Past Participle (with *have, has, had*)
1. hike	hiking	hiked	hiked
2. try			
3. show			
4. talk			
5. bring			
6. ring			
7. create			
8. fly			
9. drink			
10. witness			
11. wear			
12. catch			
13. grow			
14. begin			
15. go			
16. sit			
17. think			
18. see			
19. teach			
20. understand			
21. forget			
22. splash			
23. eat			
24. watch			
25. arrive			

Present, Past, and Future Tenses

The **tense** of a verb tells the time of the action or being.

Present tense tells that something is happening now.

Examples: Dena *laughs* at the jokes.   Jon *walks* home.

Past tense tells that something happened in the past. The action is over.

Examples: Dena *laughed* at the jokes.   Jon *walked* home.

Future tense tells that something will happen in the future. Use *will* with the verb.

Examples: Dena *will laugh* at the jokes.   Jon *will walk* home.

Write the verb or verb phrase from each sentence and label it *present*, *past*, or *future*.

1. Marlene works in her garden every day. _____

2. Yesterday, she prepared the ground for the tomatoes. _____

3. Tomorrow, she will set the plants in the ground. _____

4. She planted carrots last week. _____

5. Leaves will appear in a few days. _____

6. Marlene will pick radishes tomorrow. _____

7. She pulls weeds every day. _____

8. The garden will soon be full of vegetables. _____

9. Teddy's team will bat first. _____

10. The visiting team always bats first. _____

11. In the last game, she played first base. _____

12. Sometimes, a player changes positions. _____

13. The coach gives everyone a chance to play. _____

Write a sentence with each verb, using the tense in parentheses.

14. water (present) _____

15. dig (future) _____

16. grow (future) _____

17. help (past) _____

Perfect Tenses

There are three **perfect tenses: present perfect, past perfect,** and **future perfect.**

Form the perfect tenses with the past participle and the helping verbs *have, has, had,* or *will have.*

Examples: Mr. Lee *has arranged* a comedy show for us. (present perfect)
               Mr. Lee *had arranged* a comedy show for us. (past perfect)
               Mr. Lee *will have arranged* a comedy show for us. (future perfect)

Underline the verb phrase in each sentence and label it *present perfect, past perfect,* **or** *future perfect.*

1. We have started a reading club. _____

2. By next year, we will have discussed eight books. _____

3. Susan often had suggested the book *Little Women* to the club members. _____

4. I have always enjoyed books by Louisa May Alcott. _____

5. I will have finished the book before the next meeting. _____

6. The school newspaper has written about our group. _____

7. The reporter had interviewed us last year. _____

8. We have chosen the book *The Secret Garden* as our next selection. _____

Complete each sentence, using the correct perfect tense of the verb in parentheses.

9. Tom _____ sitting next to Francie this year. (enjoy)

10. He _____ not _____ her before September. (meet)

11. Next week, they _____ each other for six months. (know)

12. They _____ often _____ their favorite books this year. (share)

13. Francie read a novel because Tom _____ it. (recommend)

Irregular Verbs

An **irregular verb** does not end with *ed* to form the past and past participle. Verbs such as *be, have,* and *do* form the past and past participle in other ways.

Examples:

Present	Past	Past Participle
is, are, am	was, were	been
has, have	had	had
do, does	did	done

Complete each sentence with the correct form of the verb in parentheses.

1. I _____ excited about our camping trip.
   (past of *be*)

2. I had _____ a lot of research about camping.
   (past of *do*)

3. _____ you excited about it, too?
   (past of *be*)

4. Has your family ever _____ camping?
   (past participle of *be*)

5. Last year, we _____ camp outs in our backyard once a month.
   (past of *have*)

6. We _____ a lot of fun on those camp outs.
   (past of *have*)

7. Jason had _____ a great help, too.
   (past participle of *be*)

8. He _____ an expert camper and taught a camping class.
   (past of *be*)

9. I _____ fun in his class.
   (past of *have*)

10. We have _____ a great time learning how to camp!
    (past participle of *have*)

Underline the verb or verb phrase and label it *regular* or *irregular.*

11. Mr. Yen enjoyed the trip to Yosemite. _____

12. He hiked to Half Dome. _____

13. The Half Dome hike was very difficult and long. _____

14. Mr. Yen used a head lamp on his way back. _____

More Irregular Verbs

> Remember that an **irregular verb** is a verb that does not end with *ed* to show the past and past participle.
>
> *Examples:*   I *ate* at home.   I *have eaten* at home.

Complete each sentence. Write the past or the past participle form of the verb in parentheses.

1. Nancy's peach tree has _____ several feet.
   (grow)

2. She _____ it five years ago.
   (buy)

3. Another gardener had _____ it to her.
   (sell)

4. Since then, she has _____ hours caring for it.
   (spend)

5. She has _____ very good care of it.
   (take)

6. It has _____ a very large tree.
   (become)

7. Her friends have never _____ such beautiful peaches.
   (see)

8. Nancy has _____ some peaches to them.
   (give)

9. Her family has already _____ a few this summer.
   (eat)

10. Last year, she _____ several pounds of peaches.
    (freeze)

11. She _____ dozens of pies.
    (make)

12. This year, she has _____ the bruised peaches for jam.
    (choose)

13. The neighbors have _____ Nancy how to make jam.
    (tell)

14. They also _____ a variety of vegetables in their garden.
    (grow)

15. Sarah and María have _____ fresh produce at the market.
    (buy)

Direct Objects

A **direct object** is the noun or pronoun that receives the action of the verb. A direct object tells who or what receives the action.

Example: Bobby loved his *parents.*

Underline the direct object in each sentence.

1. A narrow strip of land once connected North America with South America.

2. The strip of land blocked ocean travel between the Atlantic Ocean and the Pacific Ocean.

3. The Panama Canal now divides the two continents.

4. It provides a short route from the Atlantic Ocean to the Pacific Ocean.

5. The United States operated the canal after building it.

6. Before the eruption of Mount St. Helens, people heard a deep rumble.

7. People more than 200 miles away noticed the noise.

8. Hot gas and ash burned entire forests.

9. The eruption killed more than 60 people.

10. Many residents lost their homes.

11. My dog Chester eats tomatoes.

12. He devours potatoes.

13. My dog wrinkles the covers on the bed.

14. I flatten the pillows on the sofa.

15. Silvia takes a nap every afternoon.

Rewrite each incomplete sentence, adding a direct object.

16. Ships can carry from one ocean to another in far less time.

_____

17. A Panama Canal pilot guides through the Canal.

_____

18. The United States paid to Panama for control of the Canal.

_____

Indirect Objects

An **indirect object** tells to whom or for whom the action of the verb is done.
Example: Jack showed the *dog* kindness.

Rewrite each sentence, using an indirect object.

1. Sheila told a secret to Don.

_____

2. Don gave his promise of silence to her.

_____

3. Mr. Miller was giving a surprise party for Ryan.

_____

4. He had sent an invitation to Sheila.

_____

5. Mrs. Miller handed an invitation to Don.

_____

6. Don asked a question of Mrs. Miller.

_____

Underline the indirect object in each sentence.

7. The three pals gave their guests a hearty welcome.

8. I sent my friends holiday cards with pictures of the animals.

9. My friends asked me questions about the first meeting.

10. A TV talk show host gave us a spot on her program.

11. I told her the facts.

12. A pet-supply company sent me boxes of free food.

13. A restaurant owner gave me a free meal.

14. The animals brought my family a lot of public attention.

15. My neighbors bought them new leashes.

16. The animals still gave everyone friendly greetings.

Predicate Nominatives

A **predicate nominative** is a noun or pronoun that follows a linking verb and renames the subject.

Example: Lassie has been a *celebrity* for decades.

Write the predicate nominative from each sentence.

1. Fred is an enthusiastic hiker. _____

2. He is a member of a hiking club. _____

3. Jill is his best friend. _____

4. She is the fastest walker in the club. _____

5. The president of the club is Michelle. _____

6. She is an energetic girl. _____

7. Her mother is a famous climber. _____

8. Mrs. Wu is the teacher of his art class now. _____

9. Oil painting is part of the class's training. _____

10. Enrique's first oil painting was a portrait of his mother. _____

11. Enrique will become a professional artist. _____

12. An obedience trial is a good test. _____

13. The person who observes your pet is the judge. _____

14. The pet show organizer was Estella. _____

15. The funniest entry in the show was a poodle. _____

Complete each sentence, using a predicate nominative that fits the description in parentheses.

16. It was _____.
     (day of the week)

17. The group was _____.
     (a club)

18. The leader of the hike was _____.
     (a girl)

19. The group's destination was _____.
     (a place)

Transitive and Intransitive Verbs

> A **transitive verb** is an action verb that is followed by a noun or a pronoun that receives the action.
> *Example:*   I *know* the story.
>
> An **intransitive verb** includes all linking verbs and any action verbs that do not take an object.
> *Example:*   My friends *cried*.

Underline the verb in each sentence. Label it *transitive* or *intransitive*.

1. The Mendozas went to the Grand Canyon.

   _____

2. They had never visited it before.

   _____

3. Mr. Mendoza drove the car most of the way.

   _____

4. He drove for miles through the desert.

   _____

5. The children rode in the backseat.

   _____

6. Luis saw the canyon first.

   _____

7. No one felt sadder than Roberto.

   _____

8. Roberto loved the shepherd!

   _____

9. The next day, the caretaker did stop.

   _____

10. Bobby had found a home on the prairie.

    _____

11. The workers had built a sturdy metal fence.

    _____

12. I inherited a cat from the former tenants.

    _____

13. Smith, the cat, sat quietly on the sofa.

    _____

14. I drove to the kennel for my two dogs.

    _____

15. The dogs would see Smith soon.

    _____

16. I offered the dogs treats.

    _____

17. I gave each dog a warning about politeness.

    _____

18. Then I entered the house with the two canines.

    _____

19. The cat bristled.

    _____

20. I gave the cat a hug.

    _____

21. The poodle gave the cat a sniff.

    _____

Adverbs

An **adverb** modifies a verb, an adjective, or another adverb.

An adverb tells *how, when, where,* or *to what extent.*

Examples: Our skates moved *effortlessly*. (how)

The ice is glistening *now*. (when)

The canals are frozen *there*. (where)

The air was *very* dry. (to what extent)

Write the adverb from each sentence. Label the adverb *how, when, where,* or *to what extent*.

1. Kevin rose early and watched the sun rise. _____

2. He looked up and saw billowing clouds. _____

3. They were very beautiful in the soft light. _____

4. A large gray hawk circled lazily. _____

5. A gopher cautiously poked its nose out of its hole. _____

6. Hans dressed warmly. _____

7. He walked outside. _____

8. He waved happily to his friends. _____

9. The air was quite cold. _____

10. Many people skated tonight. _____

Write each adverb and the word it modifies. Label the modified word *verb, adjective,* or *adverb*.

11. Kevin watched the gopher very quietly. _____

12. He remained quite still. _____

13. The world gradually awoke. _____

14. Singing birds sweetly greeted the morning. _____

15. Kevin heard his parents' voices and returned reluctantly. _____

16. He suddenly felt very hungry. _____

Name _____ Date _____

Placement of Adverbs in Sentences

Place most adverbs that modify adjectives or other adverbs just before the word they modify.

Examples: Clouds scudded *very* swiftly across the sky.
The sky was *quite* beautiful.

Place most adverbs that modify verbs almost anywhere in the sentence.

Examples: Lifeguards watched the swimmers *carefully*.
Lifeguards *carefully* watched the swimmers.

Write the adverbs from the sentences. Label each one *yes* if it can be moved or *no* if it cannot be moved.

1. Very rough surf discouraged most of the sailors. _____

2. Bruce can be rather careless. _____

3. Recklessly, Bruce sailed out of the harbor. _____

4. Suddenly, the wind rose. _____

5. He struggled desperately with the sails. _____

6. The largest crowds appeared later. _____

7. A strong undertow could be quite dangerous. _____

8. Our lifeguard warned a swimmer sternly. _____

9. Smart swimmers always observe the rules. _____

10. The sand grew quite hot under the blazing sun. _____

Add the adverb in parentheses to each sentence and write the sentence. Vary placement of the adverbs.

11. A wave crashed over Bruce's boat. (heavily)

_____

12. The boat overturned in the water. (clumsily)

_____

13. Bruce floundered in the water. (helplessly)

_____

14. People on another boat observed Bruce's struggle. (immediately)

_____

Name _____ Date _____

Comparison with Adverbs

> To form the **comparative** or the **superlative** of most short adverbs, add *er* or *est*.
>
> *Example:*   Bradley is *nicer* than his brother.
>
> Use *more* or *less* and *most* or *least* instead of *er* and *est* with adverbs that end in *ly* or have two or more syllables.
>
> *Example:*   Today is the *most enjoyable* day I have had all year.

Write the comparative form and the superlative form of each adverb.

1. low   _____   _____

2. near   _____   _____

3. slowly   _____   _____

4. seriously   _____   _____

5. eagerly   _____   _____

6. fast   _____   _____

7. frequently   _____   _____

8. readily   _____   _____

9. noticeably   _____   _____

10. easily   _____   _____

Complete each sentence. Use the correct form of the adverb in parentheses.

11. Leslie and Patrick practice archery _____
    than Ron and Janet do.   (often)

12. Leslie scored _____ of all the students
    in the class.   (high)

13. She aimed _____ than the others.
                          (carefully)

14. Patrick was surprised when she shot _____
    than he did.   (accurately)

15. He is strong, and his arrows always fly _____
    than hers.   (far)

Negatives

Negatives are words that mean "no." The words *no, not, never, nowhere, nothing, nobody, no one, neither, scarcely,* and *barely* are common negatives. Use only one negative in a sentence.

Example: CORRECT   No one should ever drive on ice.

    INCORRECT   No one should never drive on ice.

Write the word in parentheses that correctly completes each negative sentence.

1. On one side of the planet Mercury, the sun does not _____ set.
   (ever, never)

2. The other side of the planet gets _____ sun at all.
   (no, any)

3. _____ on this planet are the temperatures moderate.
   (Anywhere, Nowhere)

4. As far as we know, Mercury has _____ moons.
   (any, no)

5. There is not _____ who has been to Mercury.
   (anybody, nobody)

6. We do not know _____ about Mercury.
   (everything, nothing)

7. _____ of us can fly there.
   (Neither, Either)

Underline the double negative in each sentence. Rewrite each sentence using only one negative.

8. Jonathan didn't see nothing wrong with his answer.

   _____

9. We don't need no more practice with grammar.

   _____

10. I can't hardly believe you would say such a thing!

   _____

11. Rachel said she didn't have no grapes in her lunch.

   _____

12. Remember not to use no double negatives in your writing.

   _____

Adverb or Adjective?

> Remember that most words ending in *ly* are adverbs.
>
> *Example:*   Weather changes *quickly*.
>
> Use *good* only as an adjective.
>
> *Example:*   The play was *good*.
>
> Use *well* as an adjective to mean "healthy" and as an adverb to tell how something is done.
>
> *Examples:*   Linda became *well* after her surgery. The surgery went *well*.

Write the word in parentheses that completes each sentence correctly.

1. King Edward was _____ ill.
   (serious, seriously)

2. He did not become _____, and finally he died.
   (good, well)

3. His relative, William, was _____ determined to have the throne.
   (real, really)

4. Edward had promised it to him _____ before he died.
   (short, shortly)

5. The English nobles made Prince Harold king _____ after Edward's death.
   (immediate, immediately)

6. William _____ refused to accept their decision.
   (stubborn, stubbornly)

7. He _____ raised an army.
   (quick, quickly)

8. The army attacked _____.
   (fierce, fiercely)

9. Harold fought _____, but he was killed.
   (brave, bravely)

10. William the Conqueror was a _____ fighter.
    (good, well)

11. He was a _____ leader.
    (powerful, powerfully)

12. His subjects were required to obey him _____.
    (perfect, perfectly)

13. He punished disobedience _____.
    (cruel, cruelly)

Prepositions and Prepositional Phrases

A **preposition** shows the relationship of a noun or pronoun to another word in the sentence.

Example: I walked *along* the beach.

The **object of the preposition** is the noun or pronoun that follows the preposition.

Example: The sands of the *beach* were white.

A **prepositional phrase** is made up of a preposition, the object of the preposition, and all the words in between.

Example: Who lives *in that house*?

Write the prepositional phrase or phrases from each sentence. Then underline the preposition. Circle the object of the preposition.

1. Marco Polo's family left Venice in 1271. _____

2. They took young Marco with them. _____

3. China lay far beyond the eastern mountains. _____

4. The Polos traveled all the way to China. _____

5. They stayed there for many years. _____

6. Marco returned from China twenty-five years later. _____

7. Marco Polo wrote a book about it. _____

8. He had traveled extensively through Asia. _____

9. The book described Marco's travels for his readers. _____

10. Europeans learned about Asia from Marco Polo's book. _____

Underline the prepositional phrase in each sentence.

11. Many passengers leaned over the railing.

12. The ship was bound for England.

13. People waved to the passengers.

14. A few people walked down the gangplank.

15. The ship would soon be sailing into the Atlantic Ocean.

Prepositional Phrases Used as Adjectives

A **prepositional phrase** that modifies a noun or a pronoun is an **adjective phrase**.

Examples: The killer whale is a species *of porpoise*. (tells what kind of species)

That whale *with the unusual markings* is our favorite. (tells which whale)

A pod *of twenty whales* was sighted recently. (tells how many in the pod)

Underline the adjective phrase in each sentence. Then write the word that the adjective phrase modifies.

1. Sheets of ice cover Antarctica.

_____

2. The land below the ice is always frozen.

_____

3. Explorers with dog sleds have crossed Antarctica.

_____

4. An admiral from the United States explored Antarctica.

_____

5. A camp on Ross Ice Shelf was where he lived.

_____

6. The view from the boat was spectacular.

_____

7. The whales blew huge spouts of water.

_____

8. The people in the boat cheered.

_____

9. Blue whales are the largest mammals in the world.

_____

10. The trainer of the porpoises waved her hand.

_____

11. Many people in the crowd laughed.

_____

12. The beginning of each show was the same.

_____

13. The porpoises' leaps into the air were unbelievable.

_____

14. A large pail held rewards for the performers.

_____

15. Two percent of Earth's surface is frozen.

_____

16. Rivers and lakes contain one percent of that water.

_____

17. The oceans contain the rest of the water.

_____

18. The Pacific is the largest ocean on Earth.

_____

Prespositional Phrases Used as Adverbs

A **prepositional phrase** that modifies a verb, an adjective, or an adverb is an **adverb phrase**. An adverb phrase tells *how, when, where,* or *how often*.

Examples: The porpoises performed *with ease.* (tells how)

Shows begin *on the hour.* (tells when)

The porpoises swim *in a large tank.* (tells where)

They are rewarded *after each trick.* (tells how often)

Underline the adverb phrase in each sentence. Then write the word modified by the adverb phrase. Label that word *verb*, *adjective*, or *adverb*.

1. Sam Adams supported the American Revolution with enthusiasm.

   _____

2. He spoke against the English king.

   _____

3. Sam would not ride a horse, so he traveled on foot.

   _____

4. He walked far from his home, giving speeches.

   _____

5. This revolutionary was enthusiastic about freedom.

   _____

6. Whales are the largest mammals that live on Earth.

   _____

7. The whale we saw in the picture is a blue whale.

   _____

8. Whales behave with great intelligence.

   _____

9. A whale must breathe air through its lungs.

   _____

10. Whales can dive for long periods.

    _____

11. Oceanographers work beneath the ocean's surface.

    _____

12. They descend in small diving ships.

    _____

13. Water pressure would crush some ships in a moment.

    _____

14. These vessels are designed for quick maneuvers.

    _____

15. Some of these ships carry scientists to the ocean floor.

    _____

Choosing the Correct Preposition

Use *in* to mean "already inside." Use *into* to tell about movement from the outside to the inside.

Examples: The groceries are *in* the house. He took the groceries *into* the house.

Use *between* for two and *among* for three or more.

Examples: We divided the money *between* Ruthie and Daniel.

     We divided the money *among* Ruthie, Daniel, and Luther.

Use *different from* to tell about differences.

Example: The temperatures this summer are very *different from* the temperatures of last summer.

Do not use *of* in place of *have* when you write.

Examples: CORRECT: Joy *could have* become a teacher.

     INCORRECT: Joy *could of* become a teacher.

Write the preposition or prepositional phrase in parentheses that correctly completes each sentence.

1. Joe took a bus from the city _____ the desert.
   (in, into)

2. The ride back to the city was _____ the ride to the desert.
   (different from, different than)

3. The bus broke down _____ the desert and the city.
   (between, among)

4. The driver of a car going _____ town called for help.
   (in, into)

5. The passengers wandered _____ the many
   (between, among)
   desert plants while the bus was being repaired.

6. Joe had several juice drinks _____ his pack.
   (in, into)

7. He _____ kept them all for himself.
   (could of, could have)

8. Instead, he divided them _____ the thirsty passengers.
   (between, among)

9. He and another passenger had brought ten drinks _____ them.
   (between, among)

54

Recognizing Sentences

A **sentence** expresses a complete thought.

Examples: My father travels around the country.   The airplane has landed.

For each group of words, write *sentence* or *not a sentence*.

1. "The Fun They Had" is a story.

   _____

2. Written by Isaac Asimov.

   _____

3. It is about two students.

   _____

4. Living in the year 2155.

   _____

5. Their teachers are machines in their homes.

   _____

6. A complicated computer.

   _____

7. Ana has been telling Hakim an amazing story.

   _____

8. It is *Fantastic Voyage*, a movie.

   _____

9. To save a dying man.

   _____

10. Scientists are shrunk to microscopic sizes.

    _____

11. A tiny submarine.

    _____

12. Into a world of unimagined complexity and beauty.

    _____

13. Dangers await these brave voyagers.

    _____

14. Through the valves of a beating heart.

    _____

Write words to complete each sentence.

15. _____ study together.

16. Human teachers _____.

17. Today's students _____.

18. _____ would rather learn from machines.

19. _____ enjoys attending school with other students.

Four Kinds of Sentences

A **declarative sentence** makes a statement. Use a period at the end of a declarative sentence.

Example: Janelle is painting a picture of an imaginary place.

An **interrogative sentence** asks a question. Use a question mark at the end of an interrogative sentence.

Example: Who could ever create a more imaginative scene?

An **imperative sentence** gives a command or makes a request. Use a period at the end of an imperative sentence.

Example: Think about all the uses for artwork.

An **exclamatory sentence** expresses strong feeling. Use an exclamation point at the end of an exclamatory sentence.

Example: What a talented painter you are!

For each sentence, write *declarative*, *interrogative*, *imperative*, **or** *exclamatory*. **Put the correct punctuation mark at the end of the sentence.**

1. Look at the apes _____

2. How clever they are _____

3. They seem almost human _____

4. Do you notice anything about the biggest ape _____

5. That ape looks familiar _____

6. Doesn't it remind you of someone _____

7. Akiko has challenged me to a contest _____

8. Which one of us can create the most imaginative painting _____

Change each sentence into the kind of sentence identified in parentheses.

9. You should watch that ape. (imperative)

_____

10. It is copying my movements. (interrogative)

_____

Subjects and Predicates

Include a **subject** and a **predicate** in every sentence.

In the subject, tell whom or what the sentence is about.

Example: *One person* described her experience.

In the predicate, tell something about the subject.

Example: One person *described her experience.*

In each sentence, circle the subject and underline the predicate.

1. Amelia Bloomer did not invent bloomers.

2. Bloomers were the first slacks for women.

3. These pants were very loose and comfortable.

4. Elizabeth Smith Miller became tired of long skirts and petticoats.

5. She first wore the pants in public.

6. The new outfit was described in Amelia Bloomer's newspaper.

7. People began to call the pants "bloomers."

8. Most people were shocked to see women in pants.

9. The circus began with a parade.

10. Every performer wore a glittery costume.

11. Lillie had been to the circus twice.

12. The acrobats flew through the air.

Think of a subject or predicate to complete each sentence. Write *subject* or *predicate* to show what to add. Then write the sentence. Remember to begin each sentence with a capital letter and end it with a punctuation mark that shows what kind of sentence it is.

13. are awkward to wear for running _____

_____

14. different types of pants _____

_____

Complete and Simple Subjects

> The **complete subject** is all the words in the subject.
>
> *Example:*   *My two older brothers* stared at me silently.
>
> The **simple subject** is the main word or words in the subject.
>
> *Example:*   My two older *brothers* stared at me silently.
>
> Sometimes the complete subject and the simple subject are the same.
>
> *Example:*   *Xavier* stared at me silently.

Write the complete subject of each sentence. Underline the simple subject.

1. My best friend is afraid of snakes. _____

2. Some snakes are poisonous. _____

3. Glands in the snake's head produced the venom. _____

4. Special fangs inject the poison into the victim. _____

5. The deadly venom can kill a large man. _____

6. My brothers are acting suspiciously. _____

7. Jaime took a letter out of the mailbox yesterday. _____

8. The contents of that letter mystify me. _____

9. Two classmates of mine whispered behind my back. _____

10. This secret is fun for everyone except me. _____

11. Several members of the crew were sewing costumes. _____

12. Angelina was working in the costume room. _____

13. Many costumes were still unfinished. _____

14. Other outfits needed alterations. _____

15. Four students joined the costume crew. _____

Write a complete subject for each sentence. Underline the simple subject.

16. _____ is feared by desert travelers.

17. _____ watches for poisonous snakes.

18. _____ will avoid people if possible.

Complete and Simple Predicates

> The **complete predicate** is all the words in the predicate.
>
> *Example:*   Everyone in my house *is keeping a secret.*
>
> The **simple predicate** is the main word or words in the predicate.
>
> *Example:*   Everyone in my house *is keeping* a secret.
>
> Sometimes the complete predicate and the simple predicate are the same.
>
> *Example:*   Everyone *smiles.*

Write the complete predicate of each sentence. Underline the simple predicate.

1. Jeff carried his board toward the water. _____

2. He paddled out toward the large breakers. _____

3. A huge wave crashed over his head. _____

4. The surf tossed the board into the air. _____

5. Grandma López says nothing to me. _____

6. The secret was revealed on Saturday afternoon. _____

7. My relatives from near and far arrived on my birthday. _____

8. Even Aunt María came. _____

9. I had a wonderful, fantastic party. _____

10. The pink eraser bounced onto the floor. _____

11. Miles stared at the eraser for five minutes. _____

12. Every rubbery side stretched. _____

13. The enormous eraser bumped into the teacher's desk. _____

14. The entire class watched the eraser with amazement. _____

15. Mrs. Reyna quickly picked it up. _____

Finding Subjects of Sentences

To find the simple subject of an interrogative sentence, first make it declarative. Then ask whom or what it is about.

Example: Did *Sandra Cisneros* write that book?

Remember that the simple subject of an imperative sentence is usually not stated but is understood to be *you*.

Example: (*You*) Read that book.

In a declarative sentence that begins with *here* or *there*, look for the simple subject after the predicate.

Example: There are many *books* to read.

Write the simple subject of each sentence. Then write *declarative*, *interrogative*, *imperative*, or *exclamatory* to tell what kind of sentence it is.

1. Are the new neighbors home today?

_____

_____

2. There was a woman in the house an hour ago.

_____

_____

3. Where did she go?

_____

_____

4. Have you met them?

_____

_____

5. Here is a newspaper article about them.

_____

_____

6. Are there any children in the family?

_____

_____

7. There was a boy in the yard.

_____

_____

8. There is a puppy in the yard now.

_____

_____

9. How cute that puppy is!

_____

_____

10. Come to me.

_____

_____

Compound Subjects

Two or more simple subjects with the same predicate are called a **compound subject**. The simple subjects in a compound subject are usually joined by *and* or *or*.

Example: *Jon* and *Stacy* congratulated the actress.

To avoid repeating words, combine sentences with similar predicates into one sentence with a compound subject.

Example: The *members* of the cast were nervous. The *director* was nervous.
                    The *members* of the cast and the *director* were nervous.

Write the complete subject of each sentence. Then underline each simple subject and circle the connecting word.

1. A tornado or a hurricane is very dangerous.

   _____

2. Lightning and the force of wind can destroy a town.

   _____

3. A person, a large animal, or an automobile may be hurled into the air.

   _____

4. My aunt, my uncle, and my younger cousin saw a tornado.

   _____

5. Dark clouds and powerful winds warned them of the approaching storm.

   _____

6. My aunt and uncle knew what to do.

   _____

7. The family, the cat, and the dog went to the cellar.

   _____

8. Their house and garage were left standing.

   _____

Subject-Verb Agreement

Use the singular form of a verb with a singular subject.

Example: Leo *catches* fish.

Use the plural form of a verb with a plural subject.

Example: Leo and I *catch* fish.

Write the verb in parentheses that correctly completes each sentence.

1. Our country _____ an election for president every four years.
(holds, hold)

2. Each party _____ a candidate.
(selects, select)

3. Every candidate _____ his or her ideas in speeches.
(presents, present)

4. The candidates _____ all over the country.
(travels, travel)

5. Groups of reporters _____ the candidates.
(follows, follow)

6. We _____ about the candidates for months.
(hears, hear)

7. Unfortunately, some people _____ the election.
(ignores, ignore)

8. Only voters _____ the president.
(elects, elect)

9. The president's decisions _____ the lives of all citizens.
(affects, affect)

10. Not every citizen _____
(votes, vote)

11. Some people even _____ to register.
(fails, fail)

12. Most candidates _____ their ideas with the voters.
(shares, share)

13. Each voter _____ an opportunity to decide which candidate has the best ideas.
(has, have)

14. Anna _____ in a long line on election day.
(waits, wait)

15. Each person _____ a vote on the ballot.
(casts, cast)

Agreement of Verbs with Compound Subjects

> When the parts of a compound subject are joined by *and*, use a plural verb.
>
> *Example:*   Pluto and Jupiter *are* planets.
>
> When the parts of a compound subject are joined by *or* or *nor*, use the verb form that agrees with the subject closest to it.
>
> *Examples:*   Neither the cat nor the *puppies have* eaten yet.
> Neither the puppies nor the *cat has* eaten yet.

Write the verb in parentheses that correctly completes each sentence.

1. Jolene and her brother _____ to read about animal defenses.
   (likes, like)

2. An encyclopedia and a science book _____ good references.
   (is, are)

3. Fight or flight _____ an animal's usual response to danger.
   (is, are)

4. Shell and armor _____ good protection.
   (provides, provide)

5. Size and strength _____ some attackers.
   (discourages, discourage)

6. A snarl and a menacing look _____ others away.
   (frightens, frighten)

7. An antelope or a mustang _____ an attacker.
   (outruns, outrun)

8. Robins and bluebirds _____ away.
   (flies, fly)

9. A lion or a tiger _____ with teeth and claws.
   (fights, fight)

10. A chameleon or some fish _____ color to blend into surroundings.
    (changes, change)

11. A turtle or a tortoise _____ in its shell.
    (hides, hide)

12. Either the boys or their parents _____ driving to the game.
    (is, are)

13. Neither ivy nor moss _____ here.
    (grows, grow)

Name _____ Date _____

Compound Predicates

Two or more predicates with the same subject are called **compound predicates**. The simple predicates in a compound predicate are usually joined by *and* or *or*.

Example: We *will find* the card catalog or *will ask* the librarian for help.

Write the complete predicate of each sentence. Then underline each simple predicate and circle the connecting word.

1. The traffic light flashed for a few minutes and then turned red.

   _____

2. The cars slowed and finally stopped.

   _____

3. Candace reached over and adjusted the radio.

   _____

4. The announcer reported on traffic conditions and advised drivers.

   _____

5. Several drivers heard the report and chose a different route.

   _____

6. The three of us whispered, pointed, and made notes.

   _____

7. Twelve astronauts walked or drove across the dusty moonscape during the Apollo missions.

   _____

8. They took soil samples, measured temperatures, and tested the lunar gravity.

   _____

9. Back in orbit, the astronauts released the lunar module and measured the vibrations from its impact.

   _____

10. *Apollo 17*'s return to Earth brought the mission to a close and marked the end of manned moon landings.

   _____

© Houghton Mifflin Harcourt Publishing Company   Unit 2   Core Skills Language Arts, Grade 6

Compound Sentences

Use a **simple sentence** to express one complete thought.

Example: Objects from space fall into the atmosphere.

Combine two or more simple sentences to make a **compound sentence**. The simple sentences can be joined by a comma and connecting words such as *and, or,* or *but,* or by a semicolon.

Example: A crater can be formed by a bomb, or it can be formed by a meteorite.

For each sentence, write *compound subject*, *compound predicate*, or *compound sentence*.

1. Jesse and Carroll watched a game show on television.

    _____

2. It was boring, and Carroll felt restless.

    _____

3. Carroll likes animals and prefers shows about wildlife.

    _____

4. Carroll called Jim, and he invited her over.

    _____

5. At Jim's house, Carroll and Jim enjoyed a film about dolphins.

    _____

6. Some meteors grow hot and burn up.

    _____

7. Metal or stone sometimes reaches the ground.

    _____

8. Friction makes meteors incredibly hot, and they burn up miles above Earth's surface.

    _____

9. Some large meteors do not burn up completely; they are called meteorites.

    _____

10. Have you or Becky seen the Meteor Crater in Arizona?

    _____

11. A meteorite exploded over Siberia and created more than 200 craters.

    _____

12. A meteorite crashed there perhaps 50,000 years ago, or it may have fallen earlier.

    _____

13. The Americans and the Russians have sent rockets into space.

    _____

14. My friends came, but they left early.

    _____

15. Robin or Kelly is on the telephone.

    _____

16. Elena chose the program Monday night; Ryan chose it Tuesday.

    _____

Name _____ Date _____

Conjunctions

Use a **conjunction** to join words or groups of words. A conjunction can be *and, or,* or *but.*
Example: Palak *or* Chris has a cell phone.

A conjunction can be used to combine sentences.
Example: Janet lives in Austin, *and* Elizabeth lives in New Braunfels.

Circle the conjunction in each sentence. Then underline the words or groups of words it joins.

1. Florence Nightingale was the daughter of an English squire, but she was born in Florence, Italy.

2. She was raised and educated in Derbyshire, England.

3. Florence did not want to be idle or useless.

4. Nursing was not considered a proper occupation for ladies, but Florence was determined to be a nurse.

5. Florence went to Germany and studied nursing.

6. Llamas are quite gentle, and people often make pets of them.

7. Llamas climb easily over rocky terrain and make good pack animals in the mountains.

8. A llama is not carnivorous and prefers grass and leaves as food.

9. Sandra and Larry have a pet llama.

10. Llamas emit a humming sound, and you can hear it.

11. The llama lacks speech organs and is mute.

12. Sally talked to one expert, and he told her something interesting.

13. An angry llama will pull its ears back and spit.

14. Grasses and leaves are a llama's main source of food.

15. Llamas enjoy human company and are quite affectionate.

Rewrite each pair of sentences as one sentence. Use the conjunction in parentheses to join words or groups of words.

16. Florence returned to London. She became the supervisor of a hospital. (and)

_____

17. England entered the war. Florence joined the War Office as a nurse. (and)

_____

© Houghton Mifflin Harcourt Publishing Company   **66**   Unit 2
Core Skills Language Arts, Grade 6

Interjections

An **interjection** is a word or a group of words that expresses emotion. You can separate an interjection from the rest of a sentence with either an exclamation point or a comma, depending on the strength of the feeling.

Examples: Whew!   That was close!   Oh, no!   That is the wrong answer!

Write the interjection from each sentence. Label each one *strong* or *mild*.

1. Say, isn't Mary pitching today?   _____

2. Hooray! We get to bat first.   _____

3. Well, the team is in good shape.   _____

4. Wow! Look at that pitch!   _____

5. Hey! That should have been a strike!   _____

Add an interjection to each sentence. Write the new sentence. Add punctuation marks where they are needed.

6. That's the way to pitch.

_____

7. She missed that one.

_____

8. She'll hit it next time.

_____

9. What a hit she made!

_____

10. Look at her go!

_____

Write sentences using the following interjections: *yikes* and *bravo*.

_____

_____

Avoiding Sentence Fragments and Run-on Sentences

> Avoid using a **sentence fragment**, which does not express a complete thought.
>
> *Example:*   Tells an interesting story.
>
> Avoid using a **run-on sentence**, which strings together two or more sentences without clearly separating them.
>
> *Example:*   This picture is his it is not yours.

Write *sentence*, *sentence fragment*, or *run-on sentence* for each group of words.

1. What are you doing today?

   _____

2. Going to the museum with Juan.

   _____

3. Is anyone else going with you?

   _____

4. My sister.

   _____

5. That sounds like fun I want to go.

   _____

6. Purchased a new camera for herself.

   _____

7. Until this month, club members.

   _____

8. The photo club gave her a prize.

   _____

9. Marla has joined a camera club she has made photography her hobby.

   _____

10. Fifty prizes.

    _____

Rewrite each sentence fragment as a complete sentence. Rewrite each run-on sentence as one or more sentences. Use the correct punctuation and capitalization.

11. You have been to the museum before what do you want to see this time?

    _____

12. Some objects from the Egyptian pyramids.

    _____

13. I like ancient pottery I do not see it often.

    _____

Expanding Sentences

Sentences can be **expanded** by adding details to make them clearer and more interesting.

Example: The waitress smiled.
The waitress in the red dress smiled happily to the customers.

Expand each sentence with descriptive details. Follow the instructions in parentheses to rewrite each sentence.

1. A dog huddled in the shelter of the tunnel. (Add details about the subject.)

   _____

2. It shivered in the wind. (Add descriptive details about an item in the complete predicate.)

   _____

3. Finally, it left the shelter of the tunnel. (Add another predicate.)

   _____

4. Its shadow trailed behind it. (Add descriptive details about the subject.)

   _____

5. The dog trotted down the street. (Add another subject.)

   _____

6. The dog broke through the sheet of ice on the puddle. (Add descriptive details about an item in the complete predicate and add a second predicate.)

   _____

7. The curtain slowly opens. (Add details about the subject.)

   _____

8. I remember the drive. (Add descriptive details about an item in the complete predicate.)

   _____

9. We drove from Tucson to the Grand Canyon. (Add another predicate.)

   _____

10. The girl blew out the candles. (Add descriptive details about an item in the complete predicate and add a second predicate.)

    _____

Correcting Sentence Fragments
and Run-on Sentences

Good writers correct sentence fragments and run-on sentences.
INCORRECT: The boys were hungry we made hot dogs.
CORRECT: The boys were hungry, so we made hot dogs.

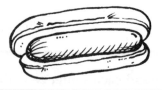

Rewrite the following paragraphs from a business letter. Correct any sentence fragments or run-on sentences.

I should begin by telling you how long I have been a customer of Ronnie's. For five years. I have always been satisfied with your merchandise and your service.

I am happy to have an opportunity to tell you how much I have enjoyed shopping at Ronnie's. However, my letter has a different purpose. To ask you to carry my favorite line of sporting goods. Sporty's. I have begun shopping elsewhere for sporting goods. I would rather be shopping at Ronnie's it is my favorite store. Besides, your other customers would enjoy Sporty's top-quality goods. Available at Ronnie's low prices.

Please consider my suggestion let me know what you decide.

_____

_____

_____

_____

_____

_____

_____

_____

_____

_____

_____

_____

Phrases and Clauses

A **phrase** is a group of words that work together. A phrase does not have both a subject and a predicate.

Example: from the kitchen window

A **clause** is a group of words that has a subject and a predicate. Some clauses can stand alone as sentences; others cannot.

Example: Everyone should know about medical emergencies.

Write *phrase* or *clause* to identify each group of words.

1. we enjoy living in this town _____

2. near friendly, helpful neighbors _____

3. from the nearest ocean _____

4. since they moved to Ohio _____

5. between a rushing stream and a grassy slope _____

6. we built a cabin _____

7. from fragrant pine logs _____

8. in the huge stone fireplace _____

9. you can read first-aid manuals _____

10. although my aunt does not have a medical degree _____

11. while Eric played outside _____

12. in Joseph's construction site _____

13. she saved someone's life _____

Complete each sentence. Add the kind of word group named in parentheses.

14. When I grow up, _____.
                              (clause)

15. I want to live _____.
                          (phrase)

16. _____, I will study this weekend.
        (clause)

17. After he examined Leah, the doctor said, "You have been bitten _____."
                                                                         (phrase)

Independent and Dependent Clauses

An **independent clause** expresses a complete thought and can stand alone as a simple sentence.

Examples: *Some pollution affects our homes and schools.*

If their neighbors cooperate, *young people and adults can clean up their neighborhoods.*

A **dependent clause** contains a subject and predicate, but it does not express a complete thought, and it cannot stand alone.

Example: People became more sensitive to pollution problems *after they learned about toxic waste.*

In each sentence, circle the independent clause. Underline the dependent clause. Write the word that begins each dependent clause.

1. Cleopatra lived in ancient Egypt, which she ruled.

   _____

2. She ruled with her brother until he seized the throne.

   _____

3. She regained her throne because Julius Caesar helped her.

   _____

4. Mark Antony ruled Rome after Caesar died.

   _____

5. Antony went to Egypt, where he lived for several years.

   _____

6. Antony and Cleopatra died when a Roman army attacked Egypt.

   _____

7. If you go to New York City, consider a visit to Brooklyn.

   _____

8. Fifteen teenagers there gained some fame because they were pollution fighters.

   _____

9. They chose the name Toxic Avengers, which was borrowed from a pollution-fighting superhero.

   _____

10. Although it was located next to a school, the Radiac Research Corporation was storing large amounts of medical waste.

    _____

11. When the Toxic Avengers heard about this, they planned a response.

    _____

12. When a crowd gathered for a public rally, the teens told the people about Radiac.

    _____

13. Public awareness grew after the rally was held.

    _____

Compound and Complex Sentences

A **compound sentence** consists of two or more independent clauses.

Example: Fires are dangerous, and they cause great damage.

A **complex sentence** consists of an independent clause and at least one dependent clause. Dependent clauses often tell *why, when, where, what,* or *which one.*

A dependent clause that begins a sentence is usually followed by a comma.

Example: *Because someone had been careless with matches,* a fire started at the Johnsons' home. (tells *why*)

A dependent clause that comes at the end of the sentence is usually not preceded by a comma.

Example: Smoke filled the house *as firefighters arrived.* (tells *when*)

When a dependent clause comes in the middle of a sentence, it is usually set off by commas.

Example: The fire, *which we saw spreading rapidly,* shot sparks into the sky. (tells *which one*)

Write *compound* or *complex* to identify each sentence.

1. Aristotle lived in ancient Greece, and he became a great philosopher.

   _____

2. Since philosophers enjoy thinking about life, they also enjoy discussing it with others.

   _____

3. Because Plato was a famous philosopher, Aristotle attended his school.

   _____

4. Aristotle became famous himself, and many people studied his work.

   _____

5. Aristotle taught Alexander the Great before Alexander became king of Macedonia.

   _____

6. Aristotle started his own school when he received money from Alexander.

   _____

7. *Tsunami* is a Japanese word for tidal wave, but these waves occur around the world.

   _____

8. Some tidal waves begin after an earthquake occurs.

   _____

9. The worst recorded earthquake in history took place in 1201, and about one million people died.

   _____

10. Earthquakes are measured using a scale that was devised by Charles Richter and Beno Gutenberg.

    _____

Vary Sentence Patterns

Now that you know how to write a variety of sentences, mix them up in your writing so that your readers stay interested. You can start with a couple of short sentences to grab their interest, and then use longer sentences to add detail about the scene or characters. Include phrases and clauses in your writing.

Example: Mr. Harvey lives on a farm. He works hard to make a living. He must know which crops to plant, how often to till the soil, and how to prevent insects from eating his plants.

The first sentence above introduces Mr. Harvey and tells where he lives. The second sentence tells something about his life. The third sentence explains why Mr. Harvey works hard. You could make the story even more interesting by adding dialogue between Mr. Harvey and his neighbors about the weather, what to plant, or how much money they could make selling their crops.

Use the first sentence below to start a story about a girl named Clarissa. Fill in the blanks to create a story about her. Think about how to keep your readers interested.

Clarissa is _____ years old. She lives with her _____ and

_____ in _____. Every morning, she _____,

and after school she likes to _____. She and her best friend,

_____, often spend the weekends _____. They also like

to _____.

Continue the story about Clarissa on the lines below. Remember to vary the length and style of your sentences.

_____

_____

_____

_____

_____

_____

_____

Capitalization and End Punctuation

Begin every written sentence with a capital letter.
Example: Let's go to the zoo.

End a declarative sentence with a period.
Example: I can go, too.

End an interrogative sentence with a question mark.
Example: Can Mark go with us?

End an exclamatory sentence with an exclamation point.
Example: Of course you can go!

Rewrite each sentence. Add a capital letter and the correct end punctuation.

1. have you ever lost your voice

   _____

2. what a strange feeling that is

   _____

3. you try to talk, but you can only squeak

   _____

4. no one can understand you

   _____

5. the climbers left their base camp at six in the morning

   _____

6. mr. Enami is a train engineer

   _____

7. miles found his math problems to be very challenging

   _____

8. does the community softball league meet every Friday

   _____

9. pedro and I go to the museum in California

   _____

10. he is such a conscientious student

    _____

Commas and Semicolons

Use commas to separate words or phrases in a series.

Example: I studied for the test on *Monday*, *Tuesday*, and *Wednesday*.

Use commas to set off mild interjections.

Example: *Wow*, I did really well on the test!

Use commas and conjunctions, or use semicolons to separate the clauses in compound sentences.

Examples: The book is entertaining, and interested people should read it.
The book is entertaining; interested people should read it.

Use a comma after a dependent clause that begins a complex sentence.

Example: *After I studied for the test*, I passed it.

Add commas or semicolons where they are needed in each sentence.

1. As her plane touched down on the small runway Amanda felt excited.

2. Lucia made a dollhouse out of construction paper cardboard and fabric.

3. Her luggage was soon unloaded sorted and returned to her.

4. If you want to see her call her on the telephone.

5. Jon helped Amanda carry her gear and they walked out to the truck.

6. Ms. Rivera teaches Greek Latin and classical literature.

7. Hey did you decide to write a letter to the editor of the paper?

8. Although you may not agree I think people should join together to fight for a cause.

9. Do Noah Carrie and Katy still volunteer?

10. Many people were traveling to Dallas Phoenix and Los Angeles.

11. The weather is getting worse we should cancel the outdoor concert.

12. The pilot copilot and navigator flew us through the storm safely.

13. Oh I thought I'd surprise you!

14. Paula North is our team captain Shu Lee is her assistant.

15. Although the director thought the film was great the audiences walked out.

16. Even though the wind is light the boy tries to fly a kite.

Commas, Parentheses, Dashes

> Commas, parentheses, and dashes are all used to set off extra material in a sentence. Use a comma when you want to identify a particular person or thing.
>
> *Example:*   Ted, our star quarterback, broke his leg last week.
>
> Parentheses should be used when the sentence already contains another phrase using a comma. Too many commas would make the sentence confusing to read.
>
> *Example:*   In the last game of the season, Ted (our star quarterback) broke his leg.
>
> Dashes may be used when you want to draw special attention to an idea or exclamation.
>
> *Example:*   Our star quarterback, Ted, broke his leg—with only one minute to go—in the last game of the season.

Underline the phrase in each sentence that should be set off with a comma, parentheses, or dashes. Use appropriate punctuation to set off the phrase.

 1. The city council just approved a budget of $25 million up from $8 million only two years ago.

 2. Cecilia's best friend Marguerite found a stray puppy in the park.

 3. Last week, Ms. Ten a local knitter opened a yarn shop downtown.

 4. My mom a world-class skier has a wall full of medals.

 5. The dachshund bred to hunt badgers is known for its short legs and long body.

 6. Archie who just bought a kayak hopes to take it to the lake this weekend.

 7. Maude on the other hand would prefer to stay on the shore.

 8. Earlier this year, Magi my friend from Alaska visited Russia.

 9. The Hope diamond the most famous in the world is owned by the Smithsonian.

10. Mr. Blair who likes to play tennis also likes to play golf.

11. The study of animals also called zoology is fascinating.

12. Ocelots which are found in South America are also called dwarf leopards.

Capitalization of Proper Nouns, Proper Adjectives, and *I*

Capitalize proper nouns and proper adjectives.

Examples: November, Chicago, Republican, American

Capitalize the pronoun *I*.

Examples: I am here.   Lynn and I are here.

Rewrite each item correctly.

1. beth ann drake _____

2. president lincoln _____

3. central bookstore _____

4. waco, texas _____

5. logan, utah _____

6. italian marble _____

7. me, myself, and i _____

8. english accent _____

9. union army _____

10. american citizen _____

11. adams middle school _____

12. *beauty and the beast* _____

13. latin club _____

14. amelia earhart boulevard _____

15. declaration of independence _____

16. yellowstone national park _____

17. mexican pottery _____

18. new year's day _____

Abbreviations

Use a period after most **abbreviations**.

Examples: adj. (adjective)   a.m. (*ante meridiem,* "before noon")

Capitalize abbreviations that stand for proper nouns.

Examples: Sat. (Saturday)   Oct. (October)

Do not use periods when writing postal abbreviations of the fifty states or the abbreviations of some large organizations.

Examples: NH (New Hampshire)   NATO (North Atlantic Treaty Organization)

Do not use periods for units of measure unless the abbreviation forms a word. (in., gal.)

Examples: cm (centimeter)   km (kilometer)

Write a correct abbreviation of each term. Use a dictionary, if necessary.

1. pound _____

2. ounce _____

3. foot _____

4. yard _____

5. Maine _____

6. milligram _____

7. liter _____

8. cubic centimeter _____

9. United States Postal Service _____

10. National Basketball Association _____

11. Rodeo Drive _____

12. Old Post Road _____

13. Fifth Avenue _____

14. National Collegiate Athletic Association

_____

15. medical doctor _____

16. miles per hour _____

17. revolutions per minute _____

18. Fahrenheit _____

19. Celsius _____

Rewrite each group of words, using abbreviations.

20. Best Carpet Cleaners, Incorporated _____

21. The Farley Farragut Company _____

22. Doctor Thomas Gorman _____

More Abbreviations

Use an abbreviation, or shortened form of a word, to save space when you write lists and addresses or fill out forms.

To write an initial, use the first letter of a name followed by a period.

Imagine that you are filling out an application for a job. Write the information in the chart below. Capitalize and punctuate each abbreviation and initial correctly.

JOE BOB'S RESTAURANT

Name: _____

Street address: _____

Birth date: _____

Date of application: _____

Exact time of interview: _____

Use abbreviations whenever possible to complete the form with the following information: 120 Grant Avenue; 8:15 in the morning; The Parker School; Helena Ann Ramírez; September 8, 2014; 3:30 in the afternoon; Ponca City, Oklahoma.

Student Information Card

School: _____

Address: _____

_____

Principal: _____

First day of school: _____

School day begins: _____

School day ends: _____

Titles

Capitalize the first word, the last word, and all the important words in a title.

Underline the titles of books, plays, magazines, newspapers, television shows, and movies. If you are using a computer, replace underlining with italics.

Examples: 60 Minutes, The Secret Garden, Los Angeles Times, Pinocchio

Place quotation marks around the titles of short works, such as poems, short stories, chapters, articles, and songs.

Examples: "Little Miss Muffet," "America the Beautiful"

Circle the words in each title that should be capitalized.

1. around the world in eighty days

2. the pirates of penzance

3. profiles in courage

4. stalking the wild asparagus

5. the cat ate my gymsuit

6. "shake, rattle, and roll"

7. "twist and shout"

8. "me and my shadow"

9. the red balloon

10. the wizard of oz

Write the title in each sentence correctly.

11. The movie stand by me is one of my favorites.

_____

12. Did you know it is based on a short story called the body?

_____

13. The story was written by Stephen King, who also wrote the novels cujo, christine, and carrie.

_____

14. The title of the movie comes from one of the best songs in it, stand by me.

_____

15. Where is last week's issue of time?

_____

16. Have you read John Steinbeck's book travels with charley?

_____

17. I just found that article, welcome to Pittsburgh.

_____

18. My family enjoys watching Monday night football.

_____

19. Did you see that movie about Dian Fossey called gorillas in the mist?

_____

Direct Quotations and Dialogue

Use quotation marks before and after a **direct quotation**. Place a comma or a period inside closing quotation marks.

Example: "The truth is powerful and will prevail," said Sojourner Truth.

If a quotation is interrupted by other words, place quotation marks around the quoted words only.

Example: "Give me liberty," Patrick Henry cried, "or give me death!"

Place a question mark or an exclamation point inside closing quotation marks if the quotation itself is a question or an exclamation.

Example: "Haven't you ever heard of Sojourner Truth or Patrick Henry?" asked Marcia.

Rewrite each sentence using correct punctuation and capitalization.

1. Leon dragged the huge crate through and shouted I'm home, Mom!

_____

2. She isn't back yet Leon's brother told him.

_____

3. Oh, Leon said his brother, staring at the box what is that?

_____

4. Queen Elizabeth I ruled a great empire, Marcia said.

_____

5. She told her critics, I have the heart and stomach of a king.

_____

6. Who else had a great impact on a country? asked Terri.

_____

7. Well, Ben remarked, Mohandas Gandhi inspired a nonviolent revolution in India.

_____

8. Gandhi inspired Martin Luther King! Terri added.

_____

9. New York has a new program, Nancy said, for student ticket buyers.

_____

Appositives

An **appositive** is a noun or noun phrase that identifies or renames the word or words that precede it. Use commas to set off an appositive from the rest of the sentence.

Examples: Our steward, *James Moreno*, speaks three languages.
His home is in Rome, *the capital of Italy*.

Rewrite each sentence correctly. Use commas where they are needed. Then underline the appositive. Circle the noun or pronoun it renames or identifies.

1. The company High Flyers forgot to include instructions.

   _____

2. The Eagle our only car would not start.

   _____

3. Jim Delgado our next-door neighbor came to help.

   _____

4. Even Jim a good mechanic could not start it.

   _____

5. The starter an electric motor was not working.

   _____

6. The pilot Captain Songrossi said to fasten our seat belts.

   _____

7. A prairie a kind of grassland is home to many kinds of plants and animals.

   _____

8. Our teacher Ms. Pesek does not agree.

   _____

9. Our favorite store Video Visions has many unusual movies.

   _____

10. My youngest sister Sandra asks to go there every Friday.

   _____

Rewrite the sentences, using appositives to add information.

11. Our school is open all year. _____

12. I would like to see my favorite film again. _____

Contractions

Form **contractions** by putting two words together and replacing one or more letters with an apostrophe.

Examples: is not = isn't   it is = it's   you will = you'll

Write the contraction in each sentence and the words from which it was formed.

1. I'd like to learn to ski. _____

2. I've asked Susan to teach me. _____

3. I know she's an excellent skier. _____

4. She says it isn't difficult. _____

5. We've asked Tom and Jack to come with us. _____

6. They've been skiing for years. _____

7. I'm working at a grocery store after school. _____

8. We aren't going to be able to sleep tonight. _____

9. Xavier didn't play football today. _____

10. They'd be here if they could. _____

11. Tiffany wasn't feeling well today. _____

12. Eloisa and Pete haven't been home all weekend. _____

13. You've signed up to take a weaving class. _____

14. Lina can't close the door. _____

15. Doesn't the mural look great? _____

Write a sentence using the contraction for each pair of words.

16. should not _____

17. will not _____

18. he would _____

19. let us _____

20. you are _____

Prefixes

A **prefix** is a letter or group of letters that can be added to the beginning of a root to change its meaning.

Example: *extra,* meaning "outside of, beyond" + the root *ordinary* = *extraordinary,* meaning "beyond ordinary"

Many English words have prefixes that come from Greek or Latin. Some prefixes have one meaning, and others have more than one meaning.

Examples:

Greek or Latin Prefix	Meaning
im	not
in	not
post	after
pre	before
re	back, again
over	too much, over
un	not

Read each sentence. Write the word formed with a prefix and underline the prefix. Then write the meaning of the word.

1. Debate Club is my friend Greg's favorite extracurricular activity.

   _____

2. I have been inactive in the organization all year.

   _____

3. I thought the audience was impolite during the speeches.

   _____

4. They should not prejudge the candidates before hearing what they have to say.

   _____

5. It is unusual to have this many candidates.

   _____

6. I think Greg is overconfident.

   _____

7. He has already ordered food for his postelection celebration.

   _____

Suffixes

A **suffix** is a letter or letters added to the end of a root to change the meaning of a word. Many English words have suffixes that come from Greek or Latin.

Example: *ful,* meaning "full of" + the root word *wonder* = *wonderful,* meaning "full of wonder"

Read each sentence. Write the word formed with a suffix. After each word, write the suffix.

1. Richard looks thoughtful.

_____

2. Louise was looking at the grayish clouds.

_____

3. I think it may be a rainy night.

_____

4. The cows were restless because of the storm.

_____

5. The heavy rains will be harmful to the field.

_____

Match the suffixes with the roots to make 18 nouns. You may need to change the ending of the root to make the new word. Write the nouns on the lines.

				Suffixes				
ant	er	graph	ism	ist	ment	meter	oid	phile
				Roots				
art	attend	audio	box	capital	celebrate	contest	critic	cycle
employ	govern	human	organize	photo	radio	ski	sphere	thermal

6. _____   15. _____

7. _____   16. _____

8. _____   17. _____

9. _____   18. _____

10. _____   19. _____

11. _____   20. _____

12. _____   21. _____

13. _____   22. _____

14. _____   23. _____

Compound Words

A **compound word** is a word that is made up of two or more words. The meaning of many compound words is related to the meaning of each individual word.

Example: rattle + snake = rattlesnake,
              meaning "snake that makes a rattling sound"

Compound words may be written as one word, as hyphenated words, or as two separate words.

Examples: shoelace, sister-in-law, orange juice

Underline the compound word in each sentence.

1. Ron and Diane went to visit their great-uncle.

2. He lives in a three-bedroom house on the beach.

3. The beach is at the foot of a mountain range.

4. Everyone wanted to go for a walk on the beach.

5. The cuckoo clock sounded when they left.

6. They had two hours before sunset.

7. Piles of seaweed had washed up on the sand.

8. Ron noticed a jellyfish on one of the piles.

9. Diane found a starfish farther down the beach.

10. They looked out across the blue-green water.

11. Diane spotted a sea lion on a distant rock.

12. The shadows of the palm trees were growing longer.

13. They walked back, watching the fast-sinking sun.

14. They were three-fourths of the way back when the sun set.

15. The beachfront was quiet.

16. Diane was spellbound by its beauty.

17. Ron found an old inner tube.

18. They sat down to read the newspaper.

19. Jess is a jack-of-all-trades.

20. Alicia lost her earring.

Answer the following questions.

21. A *rehearsal* is "a practice for a performance." What is a *dress rehearsal*?

_____

22. *Scare* means "to frighten." What is a *scarecrow*?

_____

23. A *date* is "a particular point or period of time." What is *up-to-date*?

_____

24. A *guide* is "something serving to indicate or direct." What is a *guide word*?

_____

Multiple-meaning Words

Many words can have more than one meaning. If you see an unfamiliar word, the rest of the sentence or paragraph can help you figure out what the word means.

Example: My mom reads the newspaper to catch up on *current* events.
The river's *current* makes it dangerous to swim there.

One definition for *current* is "movement of water." Another is "up-to-date." The words around an unfamiliar term can tell you its meaning. In the first sentence, "events" tells you that *current* means "up-to-date." In the second, the words "river's," "dangerous," and "swim" let you know that *current* refers to the movement of water.

For each sentence below, circle the definition that matches the use of the underlined word.

1. Josiah often <u>barges</u> into the room without knocking.

   a. flat-bottomed boats

   b. enters a room rudely

2. A woodpecker uses its bill to <u>bore</u> into a tree trunk.

   a. make a hole in something

   b. cause to be uninterested

3. Scientists use <u>tables</u> to illustrate their experimental results.

   a. charts that list facts and figures

   b. furniture with a flat top and legs

4. Molly left no <u>trace</u> that she had been working on Dad's surprise birthday present.

   a. copy by following lines through a thin sheet of paper

   b. sign that someone has been present

5. Mom refused to give Tim an <u>advance</u> on his allowance.

   a. money lent against future earnings

   b. move forward or progress

6. Our basketball team pulled out an <u>upset</u> victory in the last few seconds of the game.

   a. worried or nervous

   b. unexpected

7. How long is this hot weather expected to <u>last</u>?

   a. final, ending

   b. go on for a length of time

8. Mrs. Kletenik is the <u>head</u> of the academy.

   a. principal, person in charge

   b. move toward a goal

9. Lacey may <u>harbor</u> some resentment if she doesn't win the election.

   a. hold a feeling

   b. place where ships drop anchor

10. Could you <u>frame</u> the question in simpler terms?

    a. thin pieces of wood surrounding a photograph   **b.** put into words

Context Clues

When you encounter an unfamiliar word, look at the words around it to determine its meaning. These words or phrases are called **context**. When you think you know a word's meaning, you can check a dictionary to see if you're right.

Example: Josie's uncle is a *navigator* on a ship. He studies maps and uses a compass to help steer the ship in the correct direction.

The context clues "studies maps," "uses a compass," and "correct direction" indicate that a *navigator* makes sure a vehicle can safely reach its destination.

The dictionary definition of *navigator* is "someone who finds out how to get to a place."

Use context clues to determine the meaning of each underlined word below. Write your own definition of each word. Then check a dictionary to see if you are right.

1. The fishermen found that the bay contained <u>abundant</u> seafood to easily support their business.

   _____

2. A scientist is careful to use very <u>precise</u> measurements when adding small amounts of chemicals to a solution.

   _____

3. Drinking plenty of water is <u>vital</u> to good health when exercising in hot weather.

   _____

4. The boulder was an unexpected <u>obstacle</u> in our path that we had to move before proceeding.

   _____

5. A blue whale is so <u>immense</u> that it must eat several tons of food each day.

   _____

6. My uncle's cabin is so <u>remote</u> that his nearest neighbor is fifty miles away.

   _____

7. Would you like to share ideas and <u>collaborate</u> on the science-fair project?

   _____

8. Mr. Presley's long lectures can be quite <u>monotonous</u>; I found myself nodding off yesterday.

   _____

Synonyms and Antonyms

Synonyms are two or more words that have the same or similar meanings.

Examples: bush—shrub   dogs—hounds   shoved—pushed

Antonyms are words that have opposite meanings.

Examples: old—new   young—old   awake—asleep

Read the paragraphs. Write a synonym or an antonym for the underlined word in the space provided.

Annette had been ill (1) for a week. The day she returned, class had already begun (2).

She was early (3) because she had to stop at the office on her way to the classroom.

Annette had missed an examination (4). Mr. Castellanos sent her to a desk in the rear (5) of the room to make it up. There was nobody (6) at the desk to the right of Annette's, but Roland was sitting in the desk to the right (7).

The teacher told the students to be noisy (8) until Annette had finished the examination. When the class arrived (9) for recess, Annette stayed behind to begin (10) the examination. The examination was not easy (11). Annette was sure all her answers were correct (12).

1. (synonym) _____   **7.** (antonym) _____

2. (synonym) _____   **8.** (antonym) _____

3. (antonym) _____   **9.** (antonym) _____

4. (synonym) _____   **10.** (antonym) _____

5. (synonym) _____   **11.** (antonym) _____

6. (synonym) _____   **12.** (synonym) _____

Complete the chart by writing one synonym and one antonym for each word in the first column.

Word	Synonym	Antonym
13. wild	_____	_____
14. bold	_____	_____
15. thick	_____	_____
16. fortunate	_____	_____
17. mend	_____	_____
18. gather	_____	_____

Homographs and Homonyms

Homographs are words that are spelled alike but have different meanings.

Examples: The karate students *bow* to each other.
I made a red *bow* to put on top of the wrapped gift.

For each item, circle the correct meaning of the underlined word.

1. When Annemarie heard a <u>light</u> tapping at the door after curfew, she knew something was wrong.

   brightness   gentle

2. As her parents explained that the Rosens had gone into hiding, Annemarie could see that their faces were <u>drawn</u> with worry.

   sketched   pulled tight

3. Kristi believed that there had been fireworks for her birthday, but the truth was the bright light had come from the burning of the Danish <u>fleet</u>.

   a group of ships   swift

4. To disguise Ellen's identity, Annemarie pulled on her friend's necklace so hard that it <u>broke</u>, and then she hid it in her hand.

   cracked into pieces   without money

Homonyms are words that sound alike but have different meanings and spellings.

Examples: write—right   flour—flower

Complete each sentence by writing the correct homonym.

5. (air, heir) Prince Chang wanted to reward Tang for the merry _____ he fiddled,

   and before Chang could stop himself, he let slip that he was _____ to

   the throne.

6. (rode, road) A group of enemy soldiers _____ their horses down the

   _____ to challenge Prince Chang as he traveled in disguise.

7. (throne, thrown) The prince was nearly _____ to the ground and killed, but

   he was saved by Lang the archer. Later, the fortunate prince took the _____

   as the new king.

8. (sighed, side) Hostile soldiers gathered at the _____ of the river to attack

   Chang's kingdom, but they _____ with homesickness when they heard

   Tang play his fiddle.

Figurative Language

Figurative language allows you to describe something by comparing it to something else. Figurative language can make your writing more colorful.

A *simile* uses the word *like* or *as* to compare one thing to another.

Example: Sheila was as mad as a hornet when she lost her wallet.

A *metaphor* compares two things without using *like* or *as*.

Example: The still sea was a pane of glass.

Personification is a way of giving human characteristics to an animal or other object.

Example: While I slept in, the day kept marching on.

Hyperbole is a way of exaggerating to prove a point.

Example: My English teacher gave me a ton of homework.

Underline the figurative language in each sentence. Identify each as a *simile*, *metaphor*, *personification*, or *hyperbole*.

1. The new band director is as busy as a bee.

   _____

2. The sun smiled down on us this morning.

   _____

3. My feet were as cold as ice when I forgot to wear socks.

   _____

4. Dwight's face was a mask; we could not read his reaction.

   _____

5. I am so hungry I could eat a horse.

   _____

6. The puppy is curled up as snug as a bug in a rug.

   _____

7. I washed my mouth out a thousand times after I accidentally tasted the soap.

   _____

8. Our committee is a well-oiled machine.

   _____

9. Maggie runs as fast as a cheetah.

   _____

10. Our apple tree is so tall it touches the sky.

    _____

11. Her anger is a forest fire.

    _____

12. The auditorium was so cold I froze to death.

    _____

13. The rays of light danced on the water's surface.

    _____

Word Relationships

Another way of comparing words is to use **analogies**. The formula for writing an analogy is *A is to B as C is to D*. Analogies can also be shown using symbols (: and ::).

Example: Cat is to kitten as dog is to puppy.   Cat : kitten :: dog : puppy

Analogies can be used to show *cause* and *effect*. A cause is an action, and an effect is what happens as a result of that action.

Example: Rain : wet :: sand : gritty
               Rain causes things to get *wet*, and *sand* causes things to get *gritty*.

Analogies can show the relationship between a *part* and the *whole*.

Example: Finger : hand :: toe : foot
               A *finger* is part of a *hand*, and a *toe* is part of a *foot*.

Analogies can show how an *item* is related to its *category*.

Example: Actor : entertainer :: eagle : bird
               An *actor* is a type of *entertainer*. An *eagle* is a type of *bird*.

Complete the analogies shown below. Identify whether each is an example of *cause and effect, part and whole*, or *item and category*.

1. emperor : ruler :: aunt : _____ _____

2. nostril : face :: steering wheel : _____ _____

3. sleep : rest :: running : _____ _____

4. wing : bird :: whisker : _____ _____

5. boulder : rock :: thyme : _____ _____

6. joke : laughter :: funeral : _____ _____

7. motor : tractor :: day : _____ _____

8. fire : heat :: ice : _____ _____

9. lettuce : sandwich :: book : _____ _____

10. drought : famine :: stress : _____ _____

11. spines : cactus :: paw : _____ _____

12. earthquake : natural disaster :: apple : _____ _____

13. tulip : flower :: dachshund : _____ _____

Name _____ Date _____

Denotations and Connotations: Word Overtones

> The **denotation** of a word is its exact meaning as stated in a dictionary.
>
> *Example:*   The denotation of *skinny* is "very thin."
>
> The **connotation** of a word is an added meaning that suggests something positive or negative.
>
> *Examples:*   **Negative:** *Skinny* suggests "too thin." *Skinny* has a negative connotation.
>
> **Positive:** *Slender* suggests "attractively thin." *Slender* has a positive connotation.

Read each of these statements about Ted's Restaurant. Underline the word in parentheses that has the more positive connotation.

1. Ted's Restaurant is furnished with (old, antique) furniture.

2. The servers are all (young, immature).

3. You can sit at a table or in a (cozy, cramped) booth.

4. The service at Ted's is (slow, unhurried).

5. Ted's serves very (simple, plain) food.

6. One of the specialties is (rare, undercooked) steak.

7. (Blackened, Burned) prime rib is another.

8. Customers (sip, gulp) their cold drinks.

Read each of these statements about Ted's Restaurant. Underline the word in parentheses that has the more negative connotation.

9. The beef at Ted's Restaurant is (firm, tough) and juicy.

10. The pies are (rich, greasy) with butter.

11. The crust is so (crumbly, flaky) it falls apart.

12. A (moist, soggy) cake is also available for dessert.

13. A group of (loud, enthusiastic) regulars eats at Ted's every Saturday night.

14. The steaks at Ted's are cooked over a charbroiled (flame, inferno).

Idioms

An **idiom** is an expression that has a meaning different from the usual meanings of the individual words within it.

Example: *Pull my leg* means "to tease," not "to physically pull on my leg."

Read the dialogue and underline the idioms. Then rewrite the dialogue. Replace each idiom with a word or words that state the meaning of the idiom in the sentence.

"What's the matter? Has the cat got your tongue?" demanded Randy. "Tell me where we are going tonight."

"Just hold your horses," said Lester. "I told you it is a surprise. It will knock your socks off when we get there. In the meantime, get off my back."

"I can't help it," said Randy. "I've been on pins and needles all day."

"I have to keep my nose to the grindstone until I finish my chores," said Lester. "Then we can take off."

"Well, get on the ball and finish," said Randy. "I'm about to burst with curiosity."

"Lend me a hand, then," said Lester.

_____

_____

_____

_____

_____

_____

_____

_____

_____

_____

_____

_____

Style and Tone

An author's **style** is his or her way of sharing ideas through writing. A style of writing can be informal, like an email to a friend, or formal, like a letter to the president. It may be playful, serious, or even scientific, depending on the audience.

The **tone** of an author's writing expresses a feeling, such as suspense, humor, or excitement. Together, style and tone create a mood for a piece of writing. You may feel very different when reading a letter to the editor about a school closing than when you read an essay about the latest clothing trends. Switching styles in the middle of a story would be jarring for the reader, so authors try to be consistent in their word choice.

Read each story below. Write a word or phrase that describes the tone of the story. Then add three sentences of your own to continue the story in that author's style.

Martha had been looking forward to this day for months. After buying her first pair of running shoes at the beginning of the school year, she had been training every week. Race day was finally here, and she would be able to not only try to beat her best time, but also raise money for a cancer charity.

Tone: _____

_____

_____

Dear Editor:

I am concerned about the pollution in our city lake. It is dangerous to swim or to catch fish, and people keep throwing trash onto the shore.

Tone: _____

_____

_____

"What are you doing?" Jane asked. Her brother was packing his suitcase. He had been quiet for weeks while different envelopes arrived for him. Every time Jane tried to get the mail first, he snatched it away from her so she couldn't see who the letters were from.

Tone: _____

_____

_____

Personal Narrative

In a **personal narrative**, the writer tells about a personal experience. A personal narrative is autobiographical, and it typically focuses on a specific event.

A personal narrative

- is written in the first-person point of view.
- usually reveals the writer's feelings.
- has a beginning, a middle, and an end.

A personal narrative should include relevant details to describe the characters and action, as well as well-structured event sequences. The actions in the story should make chronological sense.

Read the personal narrative below. Then answer the questions that follow.

The family birthday party began as usual. First, my family gathered after dinner with my presents. I was excited, but I thought I knew what I was getting. My parents had never been able to surprise me.

After I had opened one gift, I heard a faint rustling noise. I paused for a moment, but I heard nothing more. A minute later, I noticed that a large box moved! It was creepy! I jumped to my feet in alarm.

1. From what point of view is this narrative told?

_____

What words are clues to this point of view?

_____

2. How did the writer feel at the beginning of the narrative?

_____

Continue the story where the narrator left off. Think about what would make sense in the series of events and which questions the writer has left unanswered.

_____

_____

Answer these questions about the way you chose to end the story.

3. What was in the box? _____

4. How did the narrator feel at the end of the story? Why?

_____

Personal Narrative: Dialogue

Adding **dialogue** to your personal narrative can make your writing more interesting. Dialogue can show how two characters relate to each other, quickly set the mood and scene, and convey information in a more colorful manner.

Example: I called Carol to see if she wanted to go to a movie. Carol had been busy with a project all week but said she was ready to take a break. I made plans to meet her outside the theater.

Now, imagine the scene with some dialogue.

Example: I was bored out of my mind, so I called up my best friend. "Hey, Carol! That new action film just came out. Are you game for going to the 7:00 show?"

"You bet! I could use a break after this killer project. Meet you there!"

The information conveyed is the same in both examples, but the second one is much crisper and more engaging for the reader.

Use the information given to write short dialogues between the characters mentioned. Make sure the characters' words match their relationship (casual, formal, respectful, etc.).

You are going to your great-aunt's house to help with yard work. She wants to plant a vegetable garden.

_____

_____

_____

_____

_____

Your dad has asked you to wash the car before going to your favorite band's rock concert.

_____

_____

_____

_____

_____

Personal Narrative: Transitions

> To orient your readers in time, it is important to use **transition** words in your personal narrative. In addition to time-order words like *First, Next, Then,* and *Finally,* you may use phrases like *In the beginning, Meanwhile,* or *At the end of the evening.* Transition words help connect events in a story.

Put the sentences in order. Use the transition words and phrases to help you.

a. At the end of the hike, we were exhausted.

b. Around lunchtime, we stopped for a snack.

c. We started the hike before dawn.

d. First, we stopped for a quick breakfast.

e. Finally, we reached the top of the mountain.

f. Then, we got on the trail.

Sentence order: _____

Afterward	Gradually	One morning	In the first place	Suddenly
At first	The next day	Once upon a time	Initially	Then
Besides that	Instead	As soon as	Just before	

Use the words in the box above to finish the following personal narrative.

_____, I heard my alarm clock ringing. _____, I hit the snooze button. _____, I realized it was still dark outside.

_____, I was confused. _____, I realized I had forgotten about daylight savings time. _____, I had an extra hour to sleep

Personal Narrative: Descriptive Details

Good writers use **descriptive details** to make their writing come alive. Adjectives tell about an object's appearance, color, or texture, while adverbs tell how an action is completed.

Examples: Iona has a new car.
Iona's new convertible is candy-apple red and has black stripes down the sides.
Jim wrote a letter.
Jim hastily composed a letter to the editor protesting the traffic in his neighborhood.

Before you begin writing a personal narrative, think about the senses associated with your story. Can you smell Grandma's apple pie baking? Can you hear the crunch of fall leaves underfoot? Can you see the sun glinting off the swimming pool on a hot summer day?

For each phrase listed below, write a few words that come to mind. Then write a full sentence that might be used in a personal narrative.

1. winter coat _____

    _____

2. soccer game _____

    _____

3. photo album _____

    _____

For each verb listed below, write three adverbs that might modify it. Then, write a full sentence that might be used in a personal narrative.

4. laugh _____

    _____

5. jog _____

    _____

6. study _____

    _____

Name ____________________ Date ____________

Personal Narrative: Proofreading

To be a good proofreader, look for one type of error at a time. For example, proofread once for capitalization errors, once for punctuation errors, and once for spelling errors.

PROOFREADER'S MARKS

≡ Capitalize.	⌃ Replace something.
⊙ Add a period.	∿ Transpose.
∧ Add something.	○ Spell correctly.
∧ Add a comma.	¶ Indent paragraph.
∨∨ Add quotation marks.	/ Make a lowercase letter.
Cut something.	

Proofread the personal narrative, paying special attention to spelling. Use the Proofreader's Marks to correct as many errors as possible. Rewrite the misspelled words correctly below the personal narrative.

What an amazing experience my bothers and I had with the wind last autunm! We had driven with our parents to Point Reyes, north of San francisco. Point Reyes is known as one of the windyest spots in the cuontry, and on that day the winds were raging up to 50 miles an hour all along the California coast.

I had no way of determining the speed of the wind at Point reyes that afternoon. I can only tell you that when we jumped into the air, we were blown a full five feet before landing The wind picked us up and carried us with the force of rushhing water. we simpply could not fall backward. The wind was so strong that we could lean back against it and let it support us as firmly as a brick wall would. My brothers and I decided to take a short walk downwind along the beach. We allowed the wind to push us along at a rappid pace. For a while, we stoped walking altogether. We simply jumped into the air, let ourselves be blown along like empty milk cartoons, and landed. Then, we jumped into the air again. Borne by the wind, we progressed as quickly as if we had been walking

1. ____________________
2. ____________________
3. ____________________
4. ____________________
5. ____________________
6. ____________________
7. ____________________
8. ____________________
9. ____________________

Personal Narrative: Graphic Organizer

Write a personal narrative about something you do well. Use the graphic organizer to plan your personal narrative.

What are you going to write about?

Tell what your skill is, how you learned it, and when you use it.

Tell how your skill makes your life more interesting.

Personal Narrative: Writing

Tips for Writing a Personal Narrative

- Write from your point of view. Use the words *I* and *my* to show your readers that this is your story.
- Think about what you want to tell your readers.
- Organize your ideas into a beginning, middle, and end.
- Write an interesting introduction that "grabs" your readers.
- Write an ending for your story.

Write a personal narrative about something you do well. Use the graphic organizer on page 102 as a guide for writing. Be sure to proofread your writing.

_____

_____

_____

_____

_____

_____

_____

_____

_____

_____

_____

_____

_____

_____

_____

_____

_____

Descriptive Paragraph

A **descriptive paragraph** appeals to the reader's senses of sight, hearing, smell, touch, and taste. In a few words, it paints a picture of a subject.

Read the paragraph. Underline the topic sentence. Then complete the items below.

The room had clearly been ransacked. The drawers of the dresser next to the window were open and empty. A trail of assorted clothing led to the closet. The closet stood empty, its contents strewn across the bed and the floor. Glass from a broken perfume bottle crunched loudly underfoot, the fragrance of its contents mixing with the smell of the garlic. The only item left undisturbed was a portrait on the wall over the bed. Its subject, a solemn young woman, stared thoughtfully into the room, like a silent witness to the recent crime.

1. List at least five words or phrases the writer uses to appeal to your senses. After each word or phrase, tell which sense it is: *sight, hearing, smell,* or *touch*.

_____

_____

_____

_____

_____

2. Is this paragraph written in space order or in time order?

_____

3. What words does the writer use that indicate this type of order?

_____

Descriptive Paragraph: Proofreading

> To be a good proofreader, look for one type of error at a time. For example, proofread once for capitalization errors, once for punctuation errors, and once for spelling errors.
>
> ### PROOFREADER'S MARKS
> ≡ Capitalize.   ⌃ Replace something.
> ⊙ Add a period.   ⁊ Transpose.
> ∧ Add something.   ◯ Spell correctly.
> ⩲ Add a comma.   ⁋ Indent paragraph.
> ˅˅ Add quotation marks.   / Make a lowercase letter.
> ✐ Cut something.

Proofread the description, paying special attention to the capitalization and end punctuation of sentences. Use the Proofreader's Marks to correct as many errors as possible. Rewrite the misspelled words correctly below the paragraph.

A set of smooth stone steps lead up to a flat clearing in the forest Here, the sun's rays filtered down through the branches of the towering pines, and the ground was covered with fragrent green pine needles. the carpet of needles felt thick and soft under Nina's feet.

a gentle breeze rustled the branches Nina inhaled the scent of the pines as it drifted on the breeze. mignled with the scent of pine was the smell of the pale green moses growing on the north sides of the trees.

What was that in the middel of the clearing Nina saw a large stump, just under three feat tall and a full three feet in diameter. four smaller stumps were aranged around it Paul was already seated on one of the smaller stumps, and the large stump was clearly just the right hieght for a table.

On the large stump lay a basket of jiucy blackberries, a canteen, and two shiny metal cups Paul looked up at Nina and asked, "Are you ready for a treat?"

1. _____   6. _____
2. _____   7. _____
3. _____   8. _____
4. _____   9. _____
5. _____

Descriptive Paragraph: Graphic Organizer

To describe something, a writer tells what he or she sees, hears, feels, tastes, and smells. The writer uses interesting words. Describe a favorite relative. Use the graphic organizer to plan your descriptive paragraph. Which relative will you describe? Write his or her name in the circle. Then write words that describe this relative on the lines. Draw a picture of the person.

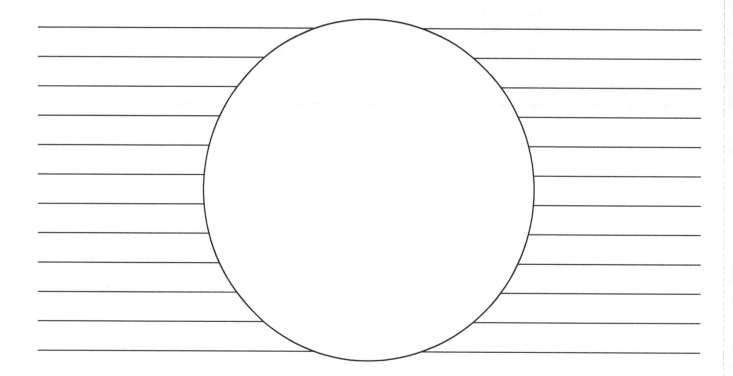

Descriptive Paragraph: Writing

Tips for Writing a Descriptive Paragraph

- Use your voice when you write. That means you should use your special way of expressing yourself.

- Help readers see, smell, taste, feel, and hear what you are writing about.

- Use interesting words to help you describe.

- Use similes and metaphors to help your readers imagine what you are writing about.

Describe a favorite relative. Use the graphic organizer on page 106 as a guide for writing. Be sure to proofread your writing.

_____

_____

_____

_____

_____

_____

_____

_____

_____

_____

_____

_____

_____

_____

_____

_____

_____

How-to Paragraph

A **how-to paragraph**

• tells how to do something.

• has a topic sentence and detail sentences.

• tells what materials to use and what steps to follow.

Put these sentences in order to make a logical how-to paragraph.

1. Boil the ginger, letting the water evaporate until only one cup of water remains.

2. You will need a fresh ginger root, three cups of water, a knife, and a glass pot or kettle.

3. If you ever need to warm your body when you are chilled, you should try making some ginger tea.

4. First, put three cups of water into the glass pot.

5. Next, cut six slices of ginger root. The slices should be $\frac{1}{8}$- to $\frac{1}{4}$-inch thick.

6. Strain the ginger tea into a cup. Drink it hot.

7. Add the ginger to the water in the pot.

Sentence order: _____

Now write 5–7 steps for your own how-to paragraph telling how to do one of the following: prepare your favorite breakfast, pick out a puppy, or write a thank-you note.

_____

_____

_____

_____

_____

_____

_____

_____

_____

How-to Paragraph: Transitions

Transitions help tie together the parts of a piece of writing. This is especially important when you are describing anything that requires steps, from cooking food to building a birdhouse. You can use simple transition words such as *First, Next,* and *Then,* but you can also use words that remind the reader where she is in the sequence of actions. Suppose you are trying to follow a recipe for soup, and you look away from the cookbook to stir the pot. You will appreciate it if the author has clearly noted the words "After you stir the pot" so you know where to look for the next step!

Use transition words such as *After, Before, During, Immediately, Next, When, Once,* and *Later* to create a logical flow between the steps in this activity.

Buying the Perfect Shoes

Suppose you have a special event coming up, and you need a new pair of shoes!

_____ you go to the store, think about the type of shoes

you will need. _____, look for the right kind of store by

asking friends or searching the Internet. _____, take the

right style and thickness of socks with you. _____ you get

to the store, ask a clerk to help measure your feet. _____ you find a style you like,

ask the clerk to find the shoe in your size. _____ the visit, you should walk around

long enough to make sure the shoes are comfortable. Don't forget to look in the mirror!

Now think of another activity that takes several steps, such as bathing a dog, building a fire, or writing an essay. Write 5–7 steps explaining this activity. Use transitions to connect the steps.

_____

_____

_____

_____

_____

How-to Paragraph: Style

Style in a how-to paragraph is usually quite formal since you want your audience to be careful with the steps of the activity you are instructing them how to do. Think of a book explaining how to construct a complicated electrical system. If the author had written the steps as though he was sending a series of chatty text messages to a buddy, someone might get hurt trying to follow the directions! Now think of a cookbook. Recipes require precise measurements, especially when using spices or other foods with strong flavors.

Revise the following instructions to establish a more formal tone. Be as precise as possible.

French Onion Soup

Cooking time: a pretty long time
Serves: a family
Ingredients: a few onions, some cheese, a container of broth, some butter, garlic, a few pieces of toast

1. Cook the onions in the butter until tender.

2. Throw the garlic into the pan.

3. Boil the broth with everything else.

4. Put the cheese in the bowls.

5. Fill them with soup.

6. Put the toast on top and then more cheese.

How to Pass a Math Test

Passing a math test can be hard if you don't get it. When your teacher says there is a test coming, go talk to her and see if she can help. Then ask your friends if they know it better than you. At home, get everyone to leave you alone so you can study. Don't watch your shows the night before the test. Eat something good that morning. Then you should pass!

How-to Paragraph: Proofreading

To be a good proofreader, look for one type of error at a time. For example, proofread once for capitalization errors, once for punctuation errors, and once for spelling errors.

PROOFREADER'S MARKS

≡ Capitalize.
⊙ Add a period.
∧ Add something.
⋏ Add a comma.
˅˅ Add quotation marks.
⌐ Cut something.

⌒ Replace something.
∿ Transpose.
◯ Spell correctly.
Ⴙ Indent paragraph.
/ Make a lowercase letter.

Proofread the how-to paragraphs below, paying special attention to commas. Use the Proofreader's Marks to correct as many errors as possible. Rewrite the misspelled words correctly under the story.

With the help of a little tuna fish and some acting skill, you can easily get your dog Titan to take his pill. As you know, Titan often begs for tunna but you never give him any. If you suddenly offer Titan some tuna with the pill inside it, he will become suspisious and refuse eat it. Try this method instead.

Make a small ball of tuna arund Titan's pill. Put the tuna ball on a plate. Then, find sumthing you like to eat and put that on the plate, too. Take your plate and sit down at the kitchen table.

Titan will probably be watching you carfully but you should ignore him. He's a very smart dog and it will not be easy to full him. your chances of sucess are best if you if just pretend you don't see him. Titan will soon sit biside you, and start to beg. Eat your own food and continue to ignore Titan. Then, very causally, allow the ball of tuna to fall to the floor. You should make a quick grab for the tuna but you must be sure that Titan gets to it first. Titan will eagerly gulp the tuna—and the pill.

1. _____
2. _____
3. _____
4. _____
5. _____

6. _____
7. _____
8. _____
9. _____

How-to Paragraph: Graphic Organizer

Think about your favorite park or restaurant. Write a how-to paragraph telling someone how to get there from your house. Use the graphic organizer to help you write.

Writing Plan

Name the place for which you will write directions.

Draw a map showing major landmarks near your house and the destination and label the streets. Draw arrows showing which ways to turn.

Write the steps someone should follow in order. Number the steps. Add headings to help the reader, such as "Leaving My Neighborhood" and "Finding a Parking Place."

Write some sequence words that help the reader know what to do.

How-to Paragraph: Writing

Tips for Writing a How-to Paragraph

- Choose one thing to teach someone.

- Focus on a plan.
  1. Think of all the materials someone will need.
  2. Think of all the steps someone will follow.

- Use sequence words and precise language in your directions.

- Provide a concluding statement.

Think about your favorite park or restaurant. Write a how-to paragraph telling someone how to get there from your house. Use the graphic organizer on page 112 as a guide for writing. Be sure to proofread your writing.

_____

_____

_____

_____

_____

_____

_____

_____

_____

_____

_____

_____

_____

_____

_____

_____

Compare and Contrast Paragraph

A **compare and contrast paragraph**

- tells about the similarities or differences of two or more items.

- uses transition words and phrases for comparison, such as *in addition, also, furthermore, likewise,* and *similarly.*

- uses transition words and phrases for contrast, such as *instead, on the other hand, nevertheless,* and *however.*

Read each paragraph. Label it *compare* **or** *contrast.* **Circle the names of the two items being compared or contrasted. Underline the transition words and phrases that signal similarity or difference.**

1.   The new house was similar to the old house in some ways. Like the old house, it had three bedrooms. In addition, both houses had two bathrooms. They also both had fireplaces in the living room. Furthermore, the old house had a separate dining room, and so did the new house.

_____

2.   The new house looked and felt different from the old house, and Janet did not know if she liked it as much. The old house was nearly one hundred years old. The new house, on the other hand, had just been built. Unlike the old two-story house, the new house was all on one level. The hardwood floors at the old house could be seen beneath the old-fashioned rugs. However, wall-to-wall carpet covered the floors of the new house.

_____

Use the information in the paragraphs above to complete the chart. Write the different characteristics of each house in the correct column. In the middle column, write the characteristics that both houses share.

Old House	Both	New House
_____	_____	_____
_____	_____	_____
_____	_____	_____

Compare and Contrast Paragraph: Proofreading

To be a good proofreader, look for one type of error at a time. For example, proofread once for capitalization errors, once for punctuation errors, and once for spelling errors.

PROOFREADER'S MARKS

≡ Capitalize.

⊙ Add a period.

∧ Add something.

⩘ Add a comma.

⩛⩛ Add quotation marks.

⤶ Cut something.

⌃ Replace something.

ᴕ Transpose.

◯ Spell correctly.

ℍ Indent paragraph.

/ Make a lowercase letter.

Proofread the paragraphs below, paying special attention to subject-verb agreement. Use the Proofreader's Marks. Rewrite the misspelled words correctly below the paragraphs.

People sometimes asks me who my best freind is. Truthfully, I do not know. I have two close friends, and I like them both very much.

My friends judy and Margie is alike in many ways. Both are intellgent, loyal, and helpful Either can carry on a grate conversation. Each has an eksellent sense of humor, and we all enjoy many of the same activities.

However, my two friends are different in many ways. I has more agruments with Judy. She complains if she does not like something, and she argue if she disagrees with me. Margie rairly complains or argues, so we almost never fights.

On the other hand, Judy is a more honest friend. She always says exactly what she thinks or feels. In contrast, margie never say anything negative to me about thigs i have said or done. Instead, she may say something to someone else, and her comments often gets back to me. If Judy has a complaint, she discuses it with the person who has caused the problem.

1. _____   6. _____

2. _____   7. _____

3. _____   8. _____

4. _____   9. _____

5. _____

Compare and Contrast Paragraph: Graphic Organizer

Compare and contrast two subjects you study at school. Use the Venn diagram to help you plan your writing. List what is true only about A in the A circle. List what is true only about B in the B circle. List what is true about both A and B where the circles overlap. Add transitions, such as *However* and *Instead*, to smoothly link your contrasting statements in the A and B circles. In the overlapping space, list transitions that show similarities, like *Also* and *In addition*.

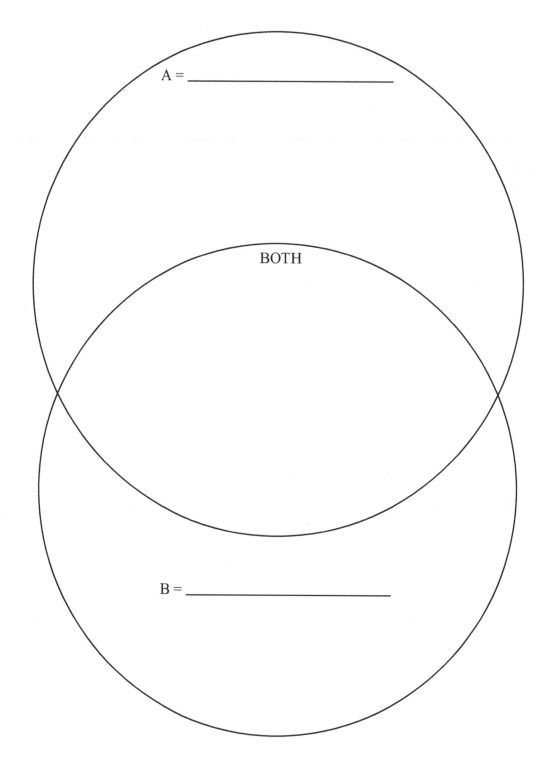

A = _____

BOTH

B = _____

Compare and Contrast Paragraph: Writing

Tips for Writing a Compare and Contrast Paragraph

- Find information about your subjects.

- Organize the information you find into main ideas.

- Use details to explain each main idea.

- Explain how the subjects are alike.

- Use transition words and phrases to smoothly compare your subjects, such as *Likewise, Similarly,* and *In addition*.

- Explain how the subjects are different.

- Use transition words and phrases to smoothly contrast your subjects, such as *However, Instead,* and *In contrast*.

- Use your last paragraph to summarize your main ideas in a new way.

Compare and contrast two subjects you study at school. Use the Venn diagram on page 116 as a guide for writing. Be sure to proofread your writing.

_____

_____

_____

_____

_____

_____

_____

_____

_____

_____

_____

Persuasive Essay

A **persuasive essay** gives an opinion or presents an argument about an issue. It gives facts and reasons from credible sources to back up the opinion.

Writers will often use some of the following persuasive techniques in a persuasive essay.

- **Testimonial** uses a famous person to endorse a product.
- **Emotional words** make people feel certain emotions.
- **Bandwagon** uses the argument that a person should believe or do something because everyone else does.
- **Hasty generalization** uses a small sample to support a conclusion.

Read the following statements from a persuasive essay. Use the word or words in the box to identify the type of persuasive technique used in each statement.

testimonial	emotional words	hasty generalization	bandwagon

1. We have to keep greedy builders from gobbling up our wilderness to make a buck.

   _____

2. Jack Tenor, the famous athlete, says that they passed a similar law in his town.

   _____

3. Join the thousands of people all over the country who are demanding laws to restrict building in their area.

   _____

4. Since my neighbors like my idea, we're sure that this is what the community wants.

   _____

Write a statement that uses the persuasive technique listed.

5. testimonial

   _____

6. bandwagon

   _____

Persuasive Essay: Transitions

Transitions in persuasive essays are very important if you want to change someone's mind.

Your **body paragraphs** should explain two or three points that support your thesis, along with supporting details from reputable sources. Start with your weakest point and move toward your strongest. Use time-order transition words and phrases such as *first of all, also,* or *in addition.*

Example: *First of all,* students can use their phones to keep track of homework assignments. They can *also* take lecture notes and mark test dates on their calendar.

Phones are *also* useful for parents, who can text their children to remind them of a doctor's appointment. *In addition,* they could let their children know if they will be late to pick them up.

Acknowledge an **opposing view** in your essay, and explain why it is not a strong enough point to change your opinion. Use contrast transition words and phrases such as *although* or *despite the fact.*

Example: *Although* some say that cell phones disrupt the classroom, students could keep them in vibrate mode to be respectful of their teachers. The chance that a phone will be needed in an emergency is much more important than the noise a phone might occasionally make.

Conclude your essay by reminding readers of your main points. Use phrases like *in conclusion* or *most importantly.*

Example: *In conclusion,* all students should be allowed to use cell phones at school. They help with homework, scheduling, and parental communication. *Most importantly,* a cell phone could mean the difference between life and death in an emergency.

Choose a topic for a persuasive essay, such as why fifth and sixth grade should be combined, why exercising is beneficial, or why children should have allowances. Fill in the items below about the topic you chose.

1. Thesis statement: _____

2. Point one: _____

3. Point two: _____

4. Opposing view and point three: _____

5. Conclusion: _____

Persuasive Essay: Style

A persuasive essay uses a formal **style**. Since the goal of your essay is to convince readers to agree with you, you should be respectful when presenting your ideas. If your writing is too informal, such as language you might use in a text message to a friend, readers (especially adults) will not take your ideas seriously.

Example: Kids should be able to play in the park till late! It's our right!

Revised: The city should consider extending park curfews until nightfall.

Be respectful of your readers' intelligence. They may have an opposite view from you, but if you are persuasive enough, you may change their minds.

Example: Skipping breakfast is just not cool. Only lazy people can't get up in time to eat.

Revised: Many students skip breakfast because they like to sleep late. However, studies have shown that getting up half an hour early and eating eggs and toast before school can help students perform better in class.

Be sure to maintain the style throughout your essay. Conclude with a respectful restatement of your ideas.

Example: In conclusion, I am right, and everyone else is wrong.

Revised: I hope you will consider my plan for implementing a citywide bike-share program. It makes good financial sense for the city and will improve the environment, too.

Rewrite each statement using formal language.

1. I don't get why people think it's a-okay to just throw aluminum cans in the trash at the baseball field.

_____

2. Sure, it may take a few more minutes to find one of them big ol' recycling bins, but it's totally worth it.

_____

3. The league takes all that money they get from the cans to keep the fields looking good.

_____

4. And anyway, recycling is plain good for the environment because it keeps stuff out of the landfills.

_____

5. Come on, why wouldn't you take the extra time to recycle?

_____

Name ____ Date ____________________

Persuasive Essay: Proofreading

To be a good proofreader, look for one type of error at a time. For example, proofread once for capitalization errors, once for punctuation errors, and once for spelling errors.

PROOFREADER'S MARKS

≡ Capitalize.	⁄⁻ Replace something.
⊙ Add a period.	∿ Transpose.
∧ Add something.	◯ Spell correctly.
∧̦ Add a comma.	¶ Indent paragraph.
∨̈ ∨̈ Add quotation marks.	/ Make a lowercase letter.
⌐ Cut something.	

Proofread this persuasive essay, paying special attention to capitalization of proper nouns. Use the Proofreader's Marks to correct as many errors as possible. Rewrite the misspelled words correctly under the essay.

Zoos are an important to society and should receive more funding. zoos provide scientists the oppurtunity to study and work with many different animals. With this knowledge, scientists can help preserve the lives of endangerd species. Endangered species can be mated with subspecies so that they may be returned to the wild and removed from the endangered list This has saved the european bison and the Hawaiian goose from becoming extinct. The manatee rescue and rehabilitation Program is an example of how zoos help protect endangered specees. This program cares for injured, sick, and orphaned manaties at different zoos and aquariums. When possible, the rehabilitated manatees are releesed back into the wild.

In addition, zoo's also provide education for the public. Zoos have many different species of animals that are not native to the united states. animals such as aardvarks, zebras, and Giant pandas live in exhibids that are meant to be like their natural habitats. Interacktive educational exhibits focus on saving the animals' habitats and educating visiters about the ways humans and wildlife can live together.

1. ____________________ 5. ____________________

2. ____________________ 6. ____________________

3. ____________________ 7. ____________________

4. ____________________ 8. ____________________

Persuasive Essay: Graphic Organizer

Should sodas and candy be sold in vending machines on school campuses? Write a persuasive essay expressing your opinion. Remember to use transitions to introduce each reason and the conclusion. Use the graphic organizer to help you write.

What will the topic of your essay be?	What is your opinion on this topic?
_____	_____
_____	_____

Reason 1 (weakest)	Why? Support your reason. List any outside sources used.
_____	_____
_____	_____
_____	_____
_____	_____
_____	_____

Reason 2 (next strongest)	Why? Support your reason. List any outside sources used.
_____	_____
_____	_____
_____	_____
_____	_____

Reason 3 (strongest; acknowledge opposing view)	Why? Support your reason. List any outside sources used.
_____	_____
_____	_____
_____	_____
_____	_____

Conclusion _____

Persuasive Essay: Writing

Tips for Writing a Persuasive Essay
- Grab your readers' attention in the first paragraph.
- State your opinion clearly.
- Support your opinion with clear reasons and facts and note any outside sources used.
- Present your reasons from weakest to strongest.
- Acknowledge the opposing view with a respectful tone.
- Use the last paragraph to summarize your essay.
- Use the last paragraph to convince readers to agree with you.
- Make sure that your conclusion follows logically from the points presented.

Should sodas and candy be sold in vending machines on school campuses? Write a persuasive essay expressing your opinion. Use the graphic organizer on page 122 as a guide for writing. Be sure to proofread your writing.

_____
_____
_____
_____
_____
_____
_____
_____
_____
_____
_____
_____

Parts of a Book

The **title page** tells the name of a book and the author's name. It also tells the name of the company that published the book.

The **copyright page** is on the back of the title page. It tells when the book was published.

The **foreword/preface** contains introductory comments about the book. It can be written by the author or someone else.

The **contents page** lists the titles of the chapters or units in the book and the pages on which they begin.

The **glossary** contains definitions of difficult or unfamiliar words that appear in the book.

The **bibliography** is a list of books about a certain subject. It can also be a list of books the author used or referred to in the text.

The **index** is a list of all the topics in a book. It is in alphabetical order and lists the page or pages on which each topic appears.

Identify in which part of a book the following information can be found.

contents page	bibliography	index	title page
foreword/preface	copyright page	glossary	content or body

1. *All Wrapped Up in Mummies*
   By Sandy Desserte
   Impossible Press
   Cleveland, Ohio   _____

2. The book you are about to read is the result of more than twenty years of research. To gather information about mummies, Miss Desserte made several trips to Egypt and actually took part in a number of archaeological digs.

   _____

3. Suggested Readings
   Aldred, Cyril, *The Egyptians*, Thames and Hudson, London, 1965
   Barnes, James, *Land of the Pharaohs*, Jones Publishing Co., London, 1924

   _____

4. Copyright © 1993 by Sandy Desserte   _____

5. Foreword 8
   Looking for Mummies................................11
   Under the Desert Sky.................................22   _____

In which book part would you find answers to these questions? Choose from the list in the box below.

contents page	bibliography	index	title page
foreword/preface	copyright page	glossary	content or body

1. What is the meaning of *papyrus*?

   _____

2. On what page does Chapter 2 begin?

   _____

3. When was the book published?

   _____

4. Who published the book?

   _____

5. What are some other books on the same topic?

   _____

6. Who wrote the book?

   _____

7. Who wrote the introductory remarks?

   _____

8. Which is the shortest chapter?

   _____

List at least one item of information that can be found in each of the following book parts.

9. copyright page _____

10. title page _____

11. foreword or preface _____

12. index _____

13. glossary _____

14. contents page _____

15. bibliography _____

Outlines

An **outline** organizes information into main ideas, subtopics, and details. An outline follows certain rules of capitalization and punctuation.

Write *main topic*, *subtopic*, or *detail* to identify each item in this part of an outline.

I. Florida Manatees _____

  A. Where it lives _____

    1. primarily in Florida's coastal waters _____

    2. warm waters above 68 degrees Fahrenheit _____

  B. What it looks like _____

    1. grayish brown with thick, wrinkled skin _____

    2. strong flippers, flat tails, large snout, and small eyes _____

    3. 10–12 feet long _____

    4. 1,500–1,800 pounds as adults _____

The lines in this part of the outline are in the correct order. Find the error or errors in each line, and write the line correctly. Remember to indent the lines properly.

II. killer Whales (Orcas) _____

  a. interesting facts _____

    1 in the dolphin family _____

    2 wide range of prey _____

  b. what it looks like _____

    1. black bodies with white patches _____

    2 26–28 feet long _____

Research interesting marine animals. On your own paper, write an outline of the information you find. Revise and proofread your work, checking for correct outline form.

Taking Notes

Taking notes helps you organize information when you do research. Some facts are more important than others. Write down only the main ideas when you take notes.

Read the following paragraphs and take notes about them on the note cards below.

The Ring of Fire, a zone around the rim of the Pacific Ocean, is the location of a vast majority of active volcanoes. Eight major tectonic plates meet in the zone. Volcanic action and earthquakes occur frequently there. Other volcanoes are located far from the margins of the tectonic plates. They appear over "hot spots" where magma from deep in the mantle rises and melts through the lithosphere, as in the Hawaiian Islands.

NOTES

_____

_____

_____

_____

_____

_____

A tsunami (tsu·NAH·mee) is a giant wave in the ocean. Sometimes earthquakes can cause a tsunami. A tsunami can travel from the epicenter of a quake at speeds of up to 450 miles per hour, producing waves of 50 to 100 feet or higher. Tsunamis may travel across wide stretches of the ocean. In fact, a tsunami resulting from a 1960 Chilean quake caused damage as far away as Japan. A far worse tsunami hit northeast Japan in March 2011. The deadliest tsunami in history occurred in December 2004, caused by a 9.3 earthquake on the Indian Ocean floor. An estimated 225,000 people were immediately killed, mostly in Indonesia. Another 1.2 million were forced to leave their homes in coastal areas.

NOTES

_____

_____

_____

_____

_____

_____

Using a Thesaurus

A **thesaurus** is a book that gives synonyms, words that have nearly the same meaning, and antonyms, words that mean the opposite of a word. Many thesauruses are like dictionaries. The entry words are listed in dark print in alphabetical order. Guide words at the top of the page tell which words can be found on the page. Use a thesaurus to enrich your vocabulary and make your writing more colorful.

brunette   **budge**
buccaneer *syn.* pirate, sea robber, desperado, outlaw, looter, raider

Rewrite each sentence. Use a thesaurus to replace the underlined word.

1. The Ross family left their <u>home</u> early.

_____

2. The children climbed into the car <u>eagerly</u>.

_____

3. Bill Ross was a <u>beginning</u> driver.

_____

4. He had just finished a <u>class</u> in driving at school.

_____

5. Bill and his father <u>changed</u> places before they reached the mountains.

_____

6. The <u>smell</u> of pines was everywhere.

_____

7. Bill and Susan immediately went for a <u>walk</u>.

_____

8. They loved to spend time in the <u>woods</u>.

_____

9. A cool <u>wind</u> blew through their hair.

_____

Using a Dictionary

A **dictionary** lists words in alphabetical order, giving their pronunciation, part of speech, and definition. There are two guide words at the top of every dictionary page. The word on the left is the first word on the page, and the word on the right is the last word. Each word in the dictionary is an entry word.

Read the dictionary entries and answer the questions that follow.

nation	nature

na·tion [nā´shən] *n.* **1** A group of people who live in a particular area, have a distinctive way of life, and are organized under a central government. They usually speak the same language. **2** A tribe or federation: the Iroquois *nation*.
na·tion·al [nā´shən·əl] **1** *adj.* Of, belonging to, or having to do with a nation as a whole: a *national* law; a *national* crisis. **2** *n.* A citizen of a nation. –**na´tion·al·ly** *adv.*
na·tion·wide [nā´shən·wīd´] *adj.* Extending throughout or across a nation.

na·tive [nā´tiv] **1** *adj.* Born, grown, or living naturally in a particular area. **2** *n.* A person, plant, or animal native to an area. **3** *n.* One of the original inhabitants of a place; aborigine. **4** *adj.* Related or belonging to a person by birth or place of birth: one's *native* language.
Native American One of or a descendant of the peoples living in the Western Hemisphere before the first Europeans came.
na·tive-born [nā´tiv·bôrn´] *adj.* Born in the area or country stated: a *native-born* Floridian.

1. What part of speech is the second meaning of *native*? _____

2. How many meanings are there for *nation*? _____

3. What is the meaning of *native-born*? _____

4. Which syllable is stressed in *national*? _____

5. Which meaning of the word *native* is used in the following sentence?

   The native pin oak tree grows well in Texas.

   _____

6. What would be the last word found on this page? _____

7. How many syllables does *native-born* have? _____

8. Would *nationality* be found on the page with guide words shown above? _____

129

Identifying Reference Sources

---

atlas—a book of maps

thesaurus—a book of synonyms and antonyms

dictionary—gives the pronunciation and definitions of words

almanac—a book which is published each year and gives facts about various topics such as the tides, weather, time the sun rises, etc. Much of the information is presented in charts, tables, and graphs. An almanac also presents general information.

encyclopedia—a set of volumes that has articles about various topics

Books in Print—lists books that have been published about various subjects

---

Write the reference source in which each item of information can be found. Choose from the list below. There may be more than one correct answer.

| atlas | almanac | thesaurus | encyclopedia | dictionary | *Books in Print* |

---

1. **Cooking**—The preparation of food for eating by means of heat.

   Types of Cooking   **Famous Chefs**
   blanching   Julia Child
   roasting   Bobby Flay
   steaming   Jamie Oliver
   simmering   Wolfgang Puck

   _____

2. **numerous**—countless, innumerable, legion, multifold, multiple, multiplex, multitudinous

   _____

3. **cuisine** A style of preparing food particular to a region or population. Many factors affect how the food of a specific cuisine is prepared. Among those factors are climate, available raw materials, economic conditions, and religious rules.

   _____

4. **culinary** (kŭl'-nə-nĕr'-ē) *adj.* Of or relating to cookery.

   _____

5. Jessica Merchant. *Seriously Delish: 150 Recipes for People Who Totally Love Food.* 304 p. 2014. $29.99 (ISBN 0-54-417-6499) Houghton Mifflin Harcourt

   _____

Answer Key

page 1

1. Carlos—person; week—idea or thing; aunt—person; uncle—person, 2. daughter—person; Mary—person; cousin—person, 3. children—person; discussions—thing; happiness—idea, 4. family—thing; ranch—place or thing; Montana—place, 5. Saturday— idea or thing; neighbor—person; meal—thing, 6. Grandma—person; dishes—thing; table—thing, 7. Sam—person; kitchen—place or thing; dishes—thing, 8. month—idea or thing; memory—idea; veterans—person; town—place, 9. Volunteers—person; mural—thing; school—place or thing, 10. Dr. García—person; mayor—person; parade—thing; bands—thing, 11. lifeguard—person; days— idea or thing; week—idea or thing

page 2

Chart: Answers will vary., 1.–5. Answers will vary., 6. Anne Frank; parents; Nazis, 7. Friends; food; supplies, 8. years; family; attic; Amsterdam, 9. Anne; it; diary, 10. story; movie; love; courage, 11. orange juice; bowl, 12. ice cream; recipe, 13. mixture; spoon, 14. punch; dishwater, 15. friends; beverage

page 3

1. Harriet Tubman was born as a <u>slave</u> in the <u>state</u> of Maryland., 2. Her <u>husband</u>, John Tubman, was free., 3. Harriet fled from the <u>plantation</u> of her <u>master</u>., 4. The former <u>slave</u> found <u>freedom</u> in Philadelphia., 5. Her <u>family</u> and <u>friends</u> were still enslaved., 6. This courageous <u>woman</u> returned for her <u>sister</u>, Mary Ann., 7. Her <u>brother</u>, James, escaped later with his <u>family</u>., 8. During her <u>life</u>, Harriet led many other <u>escapes</u>., 9. After the Civil War, Harriet lived in the <u>city</u> of Auburn, New York.

page 4

1. painter; school; painting, 2. name; style; painting, 3. movement, 4. artists, 5. painters, 6. exhibit; paintings; group, 7. canvas; eye; light, 8. painters; way; objects; light, 9. boat, 10. painter, 11. Children; world; hopscotch, 12. versions; game, 13. town; children; board; squares, 14. stone; coin; square; foot; square, 15. paragraph; sport, 16. Diego Rivera; Mexico, 17. Mexico, 18. Spanish; Mexico, 19. Zapotec Indians, 20. Rivera; Mexico City; United States, 21. Detroit Institute of Arts; Michigan; Diego Rivera, 22. Constitution; United States; Constitutional Convention, 23. Philadelphia; Pennsylvania, 24. Bill of Rights; James Madison, 25. April; George Washington

page 5

Common nouns: generals; river; violin; tune; sorrow; song; melody; joy; place; songs; future; country; peace, Proper nouns: General Tang; General Wang; Tang; General Lang; General Mang, Webs: Nouns That Name People: generals; General Tang; Tang; General Wang; General Lang; General Mang, Nouns That Name Ideas: sorrow; joy; future; peace, The additional nouns will vary.

page 6

1. horses, 2. donkeys, 3. patches, 4. days, 5. puppies, 6. porches, 7. ladies, 8. dresses, 9. hills, 10. passes

page 7

1. women, 2. photos, 3. oxen; calves, 4. sheep, 5. Wolves, 6. teeth; knives, 7. potatoes, 8. tomatoes, 9. Deer; leaves, 10. Moose, 11. Trout, 12. children

page 8

1. brushes, 2. louse, 3. butterfly, 4. men, 5. suitcase, 6. turkeys, 7. watch, 8. melodies, 9. cheese, 10. gas, 11. cranberries, 12. scarves, 13. heroes, 14. axes, 15. blueberry, 16. goose, 17. mouths, 18. reefs, 19. canaries, 20. glitch, 21. umbrella, 22. well, 23. vases, 24. moss, 25. lances, 26. masses, 27. patches, 28. videos, 29. babies, 30. gulches, 31. cellos, 32. sashes

page 9

1. Lewis Carroll's book, 2. the knife's edge, 3. the book's cover, 4. Mayor Sanita's speech, 5. the flowers' aroma, 6. the children's bicycle, 7. the sirens' roar, 8. the rainbow's colors, 9. Chris's shoes, 10. the women's purses, 11.–15. Answers will vary.

page 10

1. sculptor's, 2. artist's, 3. hour's, 4. country's, 5. thief's, 6. Robert Frost's, 7. week's, 8. minute's, 9. weaver's, 10. Samuel Clemens's, 11. wolf's, 12. nurse's, 13. King Henry's, 14. moment's, 15. secretary's, 16. Mr. Jones's, 17. hostesses', 18. teachers', 19. women's, 20. masters', 21. workers', 22. hours', 23. oxen's, 24. spies', 25. buffaloes', 26. surgeons', 27. sheep's, 28. secretaries', 29. Britain's worst balloonist, 30. a colleague's help, 31. the balloon's ropes, 32. the flyers' calls for help

page 11

1. Luis's—singular, 2. children's—plural, 3. parents'—plural, 4. sheep's—plural, 5. deer's—plural, 6. cousins'—plural, 7. person's—singular, 8. adults'—plural; children's—plural, 9. Wilsons'—plural, 10. Uncle Bernie's—singular, 11. neighbor's—singular, 12. families'—plural, 13. boys'—plural, 14. baby's—singular

page 12

1. they—stories, 2. he—Aesop, 3. he—Aesop, 4. it—story, 5. it—donkey, 6. she—owner, 7. The owner gave the dog a soft bed and fed it well., 8. The donkey tried to make its owner treat it well., 9. The donkey learned that it should not try to be somebody else., 10. Can you write two fables and illustrate them?

© Houghton Mifflin Harcourt Publishing Company

Answer Key
Core Skills Language Arts, Grade 6

page 13

1. his; **Thurgood Marshall**, 2. her; **parents**; Marshall's parents wanted to give their son a good education., 3. her; **mother**, 4. it; **Marshall**; Marshall decided he wanted to be a lawyer., 5. She; **Howard University Law School**; It accepted black students when many other schools did not. 6. her, 7. her, 8. his, 9. him, 10. they

page 14

Suggested sentences are given. 1. it; **math, science, gym**; Maribel likes math, science, and gym, but science is her favorite., 2. he; **Patrick, his uncle**; Patrick said to his uncle, "I need to leave for the game soon.", 3. it; **baseball, soccer**; Although I enjoy watching both baseball and soccer, I don't understand how to play baseball., 4. it; **plate, foot**; My brother broke his foot when he dropped a plate on it., 5. her, she; **Anna, Lucy**; Anna said, "Lucy, you should visit my aunt to learn how to play tennis.", 6. he; **Rodrigo, his brother**; Rodrigo felt sad after he missed his brother's band concert., 7. it; **bone, rug**; My dog began to chew his bone after he laid it on the old rug., 8. it; **bicycle, job**; The old bicycle that my sister bought was in poor condition even though it had a new paint job.

page 15

1. us—object pronoun, 2. me—object pronoun, 3. She—subject pronoun, 4. She—subject pronoun, 5. her—object pronoun, 6. we—subject pronoun, 7. He—subject pronoun, 8. us—object pronoun, 9. her—object pronoun, 10. me—object pronoun, 11. him—object pronoun, 12. you—subject pronoun, 13. I—subject pronoun, 14. They—subject pronoun, 15. him—object pronoun

page 16

1. I, 2. We, 3. her, 4. They, 5. them, 6. him, 7. they, 8. them, 9. I, 10. We, 11. I, 12. They, 13. him, 14. her, 15. them, Sentences will vary. Be sure that two of the following pronouns are used correctly: *me, us, she, he.*

page 17

1. Annie Oakley was famous for her shooting ability., 2. Mr. Oakley let her use his gun., 3. Buffalo Bill made Annie a star in his show., 4. Annie never missed her target., 5. Audiences could hardly believe their eyes., 6. Jeremy wants to use your stereo., 7. The dog devoured his food., 8. The Reynas had their couch reupholstered., 9. I want to change my schedule.

page 18

Answers may vary. Possible answers are given. 1. their, 2. our, 3. his, 4. our, 5. their, 6. its, 7. their, 8. theirs, 9. their, 10. their, 11. her, 12. its, 13. their, 14. his, 15. their, 16. their, 17. Its

page 19

1. herself—Diane, 2. himself—author, 3. themselves—members, 4. ourselves—we, 5. myself—I, 6. himself—Joe, 7. itself—dog, 8. themselves—Ed and Beverly, 9. myself—I, 10. ourselves—Estella and I, 11. herself, 12. itself, 13. himself, 14. yourself, 15. ourselves, 16. themselves

page 20

1. Everyone—singular, 2. Some—plural, 3. Everything—singular, 4. anybody—singular, 5. many—plural, 6. have, 7. create, 8. helps, 9. needs, 10. want, 11. is

page 21

1. Who, 2. Whom, 3. who, 4. whom, 5. Who, 6. whom, 7. who, 8. Who, 9. whom, 10. Who, 11. Who's, 12. Whose, 13. Who's, 14. Who's, 15. whose, 16. Whose, 17. Who's, 18. Who's

page 22

1. him; some; her, 2. him, 3. She; them, 4. few, 5. I; them, 6. her, 7. He; it, 8. I, 9. they; her, 10. him, 11. herself, 12. it, 13. them; herself; she; her, 14. her, 15. themselves, 16. they; her, 17. she; it, 18. their, 19. herself, 20. she, 21. their, 22. her; hers, 23. herself; she, 24. her, 25. he, 26. themselves, 27. it, 28. she, 29. she; herself, 30. she; it, 31. me; I; them, 32. I; he; anything; it, 33. she, 34. I; her; I, 35. I; myself

page 23

1. an—article; enormous—describing, 2. long—describing; cold—describing, 3. Rich—describing; the—article; black—describing; fertile—describing, 4. the—article; early—describing, 5. The—article; a—article; sociable—describing, 6. A—article; calm—describing; alert—describing; the—article; smallest—describing, 7. important—describing; an—article; early—describing, 8. Nightly—describing; rich—describing

page 24

Answers will vary.

page 25

1. African; Africa, 2. Hungarian; Hungary, 3. English; England, 4. German, Germany, 5. Italian; Italy, 6. Tibetan; Tibet, 7. Islamic; Islam, 8. Egyptian; Egypt, 9. Japanese; Japan, 10. Mexican; Mexico, 11.–15. Sentences will vary. Be sure that proper adjectives are used correctly.

page 26

1. This—singular, 2. those—plural, 3. These—plural, 4. these—plural, 5. that—singular, 6. this—singular, 7.–14. Sentences will vary. 7. pronoun, 8. adjective, 9. pronoun, 10. adjective, 11. pronoun, 12. adjective, 13. pronoun, 14. adjective

page 27

1. warm—air, 2. sweet—flowers, 3. High—sun,
4. peaceful—horses, 5. happy—Sharon, 6. eager—She,
7. ready—horse, 8. beautiful—day, 9. skillful—surgeon,
10. bitter—mango, 11. fast—horse, 12. gray—coat,
13. silver—it, 14. unusual—Horses, 15. well trained—They,
16. brave—Rin Tin Tin/Lassie, 17. good—they,
18. fearless—Rin Tin Tin, 19.–20. Sentences will vary.

page 28

1. colder; coldest, 2. safer; safest, 3. funnier; funniest,
4. flatter; flattest, 5. shinier; shiniest, 6. taller; tallest,
7. whiter; whitest, 8. sweeter; sweetest, 9. sadder; saddest,
10. younger; youngest, 11. larger, 12. smaller, 13. smallest

page 29

Answers may also use *less* and *least*. 1. more energetic;
most energetic, 2. more difficult; most difficult, 3. more
generous; most generous, 4. more affectionate; most
affectionate, 5. more active; most active, 6. worse; worst,
7. more; most, 8. more likely; most likely, 9. more
expensive; most expensive, 10. more crowded; most
crowded, 11. Ruffles is the most beautiful puppy of the
litter., 12. Sport is more intelligent than Ruffles.,
13. Of all the puppies, Tuffy is the most playful.

page 30

1. stronger; more impressive, 2. most elaborate,
3. beautiful; greatest, 4. more aggressive; largest, 5. best,
6. bad, 7. better, 8. better; worse, 9. more enjoyable,
10. best, 11. The; fierce, 12. This; the; first; the, 13. Few;
Union, 14. A; the; Confederate, 15. The; heavy, 16. That;
an, 17. Many; both, 18. a; pivotal, 19. the; several, 20. a;
memorable; the

page 31

1. originated, 2. compete, 3. leaped, 4. stretched,
5. grabbed, 6. dribbled, 7. aimed, 8. flew, 9. bounced,
10. jumped, 11.–15. Sentences will vary.

page 32

1. celebrated—action, 2. is—linking, 3. reaches—action,
4. cooked—action, 5. appeared—linking, 6. greeted—
action, 7. smelled—linking, 8. became—linking,
9. looked—linking, 10. is—linking, 11. rises—action,
12. escapes—action, 13. are—linking, 14. were—linking,
15. was—linking, 16. study—action, 17. recycles—action,
18. was—linking, 19. opened—action, 20. were—linking

page 33

Action verbs: compete, need, carries, defeated, ran, ran;
linking verbs: are, are, is, is, is, 1.–10. Answers will vary.

page 34

1. are moving—moving, 2. have lived—lived, 3. am
missing—missing, 4. has been—been, 5. had moved—
moved, 6. do want—want, 7. has accepted—accepted,

8. is living—living, 9. was working—working, 10. did
offer—offer, 11. Does like—like, 12. was complaining—
complaining, 13. had lived—lived, 14. is enjoying—
enjoying, 15. will find—find, 16. has entered—entered,
17. might meet—meet, 18. may visit—visit, 19. is living—
living, 20. could give—give

page 35

1. helping, 2. helping, 3. main, 4. main, 5. main, 6. helping,
7. main, 8. helping, 9. helping, 10. main, 11. main,
12. helping, 13. helping, 14. helping, 15. helping,
16.–20. Answers will vary. Suggested: 16. are blooming,
17. will be, 18. should visit, 19. does need, 20. were picked

page 36

1. studies—present, 2. reading—present participle,
3. taught—past participle, 4. learned—past participle,
5. visited—past, 6. gone—past participle, 7. seen—past
participle, 8. read—past participle, 9. planning—present
participle, 10. talks—present, 11. learns—present,
12. watching—present participle

page 37

2. trying; tried; tried, 3. showing; showed; shown,
4. talking; talked; talked, 5. bringing; brought; brought,
6. ringing; rang; rung, 7. creating; created; created,
8. flying; flew; flown, 9. drinking; drank; drunk,
10. witnessing; witnessed; witnessed, 11. wearing; wore;
worn, 12. catching; caught; caught, 13. growing; grew;
grown, 14. beginning; began; begun, 15. going; went; gone,
16. sitting; sat; sat, 17. thinking; thought; thought,
18. seeing; saw; seen, 19. teaching; taught; taught,
20. understanding; understood; understood, 21. forgetting;
forgot; forgotten, 22. splashing; splashed; splashed,
23. eating; ate; eaten, 24. watching; watched; watched,
25. arriving; arrived; arrived

page 38

1. works—present, 2. prepared—past, 3. will set—future,
4. planted—past, 5. will appear—future, 6. will pick—
future, 7. pulls—present, 8. will be—future, 9. will bat—
future, 10. bats—present, 11. played—past, 12. changes—
present, 13. gives—present, 14.–17. Sentences will vary.
14. water/waters, 15. will dig, 16. will grow, 17. helped

page 39

1. have started—present perfect, 2. will have discussed—
future perfect, 3. had suggested—past perfect, 4. have
enjoyed—present perfect, 5. will have finished—future
perfect, 6. has written—present perfect, 7. had
interviewed—past perfect, 8. have chosen—present perfect,
9. has enjoyed, 10. had met, 11. will have known, 12. have
shared, 13. had recommended

page 40

1. was, 2. done, 3. Were, 4. been, 5. had, 6. had, 7. been,

8. was, 9. had, 10. had, 11. enjoyed—regular, 12. hiked—regular, 13. was—irregular, 14. used—regular

page 41

1. grown, 2. bought, 3. sold, 4. spent, 5. taken, 6. become, 7. seen, 8. given, 9. eaten, 10. froze, 11. made, 12. chosen, 13. told, 14. grew, 15. bought

page 42

1. North America, 2. travel, 3. continents, 4. route, 5. canal, 6. rumble, 7. noise, 8. forests, 9. people, 10. homes, 11. tomatoes, 12. potatoes, 13. covers, 14. pillows, 15. nap, 16.–18. Sentences will vary. Suggested: 16. Ships can carry passengers from one ocean to another in far less time., 17. A Panama Canal pilot guides ships through the Canal., 18. The United States paid money to Panama for control of the Canal.

page 43

1. Sheila told Don a secret., 2. Don gave her his promise of silence., 3. Mr. Miller was giving Ryan a surprise party., 4. He had sent Sheila an invitation., 5. Mrs. Miller handed Don an invitation., 6. Don asked Mrs. Miller a question., 7. guests, 8. friends, 9. me, 10. us, 11. her, 12. me, 13. me, 14. family, 15. them, 16. everyone

page 44

1. hiker, 2. member, 3. friend, 4. walker, 5. Michelle, 6. girl, 7. climber, 8. teacher, 9. part, 10. portrait, 11. artist, 12. test, 13. judge, 14. Estella, 15. poodle, 16.–19. Sentences will vary.

page 45

1. went—intransitive, 2. had visited—transitive, 3. drove—transitive, 4. drove—intransitive, 5. rode—intransitive, 6. saw—transitive, 7. felt—intransitive, 8. loved—transitive, 9. did stop—intransitive, 10. had found—transitive, 11. had built—transitive, 12. inherited—transitive, 13. sat—intransitive, 14. drove—intransitive, 15. would see—transitive, 16. offered—transitive, 17. gave—transitive, 18. entered—transitive, 19. bristled—intransitive, 20. gave—transitive, 21. gave—transitive

page 46

1. early—when, 2. up—where, 3. very—to what extent, 4. lazily—how, 5. cautiously—how, 6. warmly—how, 7. outside—where, 8. happily—how, 9. quite—to what extent, 10. tonight—when, 11. very—quietly: adverb; quietly—watched: verb, 12. quite—still: adjective, 13. gradually—awoke: verb, 14. sweetly—greeted: verb, 15. reluctantly—returned: verb, 16. suddenly—felt: verb; very—hungry: adjective

page 47

1. Very—no, 2. rather—no, 3. Recklessly—yes, 4. Suddenly—yes, 5. desperately—yes, 6. later—yes, 7. quite—no, 8. sternly—yes, 9. always—yes, 10. quite—

no, 11.–14. Sentences will vary. Be sure that each sentence includes the adverb and that the position of adverbs in sentences is varied.

page 48

Answers may also use *less* and *least*. 1. lower; lowest, 2. nearer; nearest, 3. more slowly; most slowly, 4. more seriously; most seriously, 5. more eagerly; most eagerly, 6. faster; fastest, 7. more frequently; most frequently, 8. more readily; most readily, 9. more noticeably; most noticeably, 10. more easily; most easily, 11. more often, 12. highest, 13. more carefully, 14. more accurately, 15. farther

page 49

1. ever, 2. no, 3. Nowhere, 4. no, 5. anybody, 6. everything, 7. Neither, Suggested sentences are given. 8. didn't, nothing; Jonathan didn't see anything wrong with his answer., 9. don't, no; We don't need any more practice with grammar., 10. can't, hardly; I can hardly believe you would say such a thing!, 11. didn't, no; Rachel said she didn't have any grapes in her lunch., 12. not, no; Remember not to use any double negatives in your writing.

page 50

1. seriously, 2. well, 3. really, 4. shortly, 5. immediately, 6. stubbornly, 7. quickly, 8. fiercely, 9. bravely, 10. good, 11. powerful, 12. perfectly, 13. cruelly

page 51

1. in 1271, 2. with them, 3. beyond the eastern mountains, 4. to China, 5. for many years, 6. from China, 7. about it, 8. through Asia, 9. for his readers, 10. about Asia; from Marco Polo's book, 11. over the railing, 12. for England, 13. to the passengers, 14. down the gangplank, 15. into the Atlantic Ocean

page 52

1. of ice; Sheets, 2. below the ice; land, 3. with dog sleds; Explorers, 4. from the United States; admiral, 5. on Ross Ice Shelf; camp, 6. from the boat; view, 7. of water; spouts, 8. in the boat; people, 9. in the world; mammals 10. of the porpoises; trainer, 11. in the crowd; people, 12. of each show; beginning, 13. into the air; leaps, 14. for the performers; rewards, 15. of Earth's surface; percent, 16. of that water; percent, 17. of the water; rest, 18. on Earth; ocean

page 53

1. with enthusiasm—supported: verb, 2. against the English king—spoke: verb, 3. on foot—traveled: verb, 4. from his home—far: adverb, 5. about freedom—enthusiastic: adjective, 6. on Earth—live: verb, 7. in the picture—saw: verb, 8. with great intelligence—behave: verb, 9. through its lungs—breathe: verb, 10. for long periods—can dive: verb, 11. beneath the ocean's surface—work: verb, 12. in

small diving ships—descend: verb, **13.** in a moment—would crush: verb, **14.** for quick maneuvers—are designed: verb, **15.** to the ocean floor—carry: verb

page 54
1. into, **2.** different from, **3.** between, **4.** into, **5.** among, **6.** in, **7.** could have, **8.** among, **9.** between

page 55
1. sentence, **2.** not a sentence, **3.** sentence, **4.** not a sentence, **5.** sentence, **6.** not a sentence, **7.** sentence, **8.** sentence, **9.** not a sentence, **10.** sentence, **11.** not a sentence, **12.** not a sentence, **13.** sentence, **14.** not a sentence, **15.–19.** Answers will vary.

page 56
1. imperative; period, **2.** exclamatory; exclamation point, **3.** declarative; period, **4.** interrogative; question mark, **5.** declarative; period, **6.** interrogative; question mark, **7.** declarative; period, **8.** interrogative; question mark, **9.–10.** Sentences may vary. Suggested: **9.** Watch that ape., **10.** Is it copying my movements?

page 57
1. Amelia Bloomer did not invent bloomers., **2.** Bloomers were the first slacks for women., **3.** These pants were very loose and comfortable., **4.** Elizabeth Smith Miller became tired of long skirts and petticoats., **5.** She first wore the pants in public., **6.** The new outfit was described in Amelia Bloomer's newspaper., **7.** People began to call the pants "bloomers.", **8.** Most people were shocked to see women in pants., **9.** The circus began with a parade., **10.** Every performer wore a glittery costume., **11.** Lillie had been to the circus twice., **12.** The acrobats flew through the air., **13.–14.** Sentences will vary. **13.** subject, **14.** predicate

page 58
1. My best friend, **2.** Some snakes, **3.** Glands in the snake's head, **4.** Special fangs, **5.** The deadly venom, **6.** My brothers, **7.** Jaime, **8.** The contents of that letter, **9.** Two classmates of mine, **10.** This secret, **11.** Several members of the crew, **12.** Angelina, **13.** Many costumes, **14.** Other outfits, **15.** Four students, **16.–18.** Answers will vary.

page 59
1. carried his board toward the water, **2.** paddled out toward the large breakers, **3.** crashed over his head, **4.** tossed the board into the air, **5.** says nothing to me, **6.** was revealed on Saturday afternoon, **7.** arrived on my birthday, **8.** came, **9.** had a wonderful, fantastic party, **10.** bounced onto the floor, **11.** stared at the eraser for five minutes, **12.** stretched, **13.** bumped into the teacher's desk, **14.** watched the eraser with amazement, **15.** quickly picked it up

page 60
1. neighbors—interrogative, **2.** woman—declarative, **3.** she—interrogative, **4.** you—interrogative, **5.** article—declarative, **6.** children—interrogative, **7.** boy—declarative,

8. puppy—declarative, **9.** puppy—exclamatory, **10.** (you)—imperative

page 61
1. A tornado **or** a hurricane, **2.** Lightning **and** the force of wind, **3.** A person, a large animal, **or** an automobile, **4.** My aunt, my uncle, **and** my younger cousin, **5.** Dark clouds **and** powerful winds, **6.** My aunt **and** uncle, **7.** The family, the cat, **and** the dog, **8.** Their house **and** garage

page 62
1. holds, **2.** selects, **3.** presents, **4.** travel, **5.** follow, **6.** hear, **7.** ignore, **8.** elect, **9.** affect, **10.** votes, **11.** fail, **12.** share, **13.** has, **14.** waits, **15.** casts

page 63
1. like, **2.** are, **3.** is, **4.** provide, **5.** discourage, **6.** frighten, **7.** outruns, **8.** fly, **9.** fights, **10.** change, **11.** hides, **12.** are, **13.** grows

page 64
1. flashed for a few minutes **and** then turned red, **2.** slowed **and** finally stopped, **3.** reached over **and** adjusted the radio, **4.** reported on traffic conditions **and** advised drivers, **5.** heard the report **and** chose a different route, **6.** whispered, pointed, **and** made notes, **7.** walked **or** drove across the dusty moonscape during the Apollo missions, **8.** took soil samples, measured temperatures, **and** tested the lunar gravity, **9.** released the lunar module **and** measured the vibrations from its impact, **10.** brought the mission to a close **and** marked the end of manned moon landings

page 65
1. compound subject, **2.** compound sentence, **3.** compound predicate, **4.** compound sentence, **5.** compound subject, **6.** compound predicate, **7.** compound subject, **8.** compound sentence, **9.** compound sentence, **10.** compound subject, **11.** compound predicate, **12.** compound sentence, **13.** compound subject, **14.** compound sentence, **15.** compound subject, **16.** compound sentence

page 66
1. Florence Nightingale was the daughter of an English squire, **but** she was born in Florence, Italy., **2.** She was raised **and** educated in Derbyshire, England., **3.** Florence did not want to be idle **or** useless., **4.** Nursing was not considered a proper occupation for ladies, **but** Florence was determined to be a nurse., **5.** Florence went to Germany **and** studied nursing., **6.** Llamas are quite gentle, **and** people often make pets of them., **7.** Llamas climb easily over rocky terrain **and** make good pack animals in the mountains., **8.** A llama is not carnivorous **and** prefers grass and leaves as food., **9.** Sandra **and** Larry have a pet llama., **10.** Llamas emit a humming sound, **and** you can hear it., **11.** The llama lacks speech organs **and** is mute., **12.** Sally talked to one expert, **and** he told her something interesting.,

Answer Key
Core Skills Language Arts, Grade 6

13. An angry llama <u>will pull its ears back</u> **and** <u>spit</u>.,
14. <u>Grasses</u> **and** <u>leaves</u> are a llama's main source of food.,
15. Llamas <u>enjoy human company</u> **and** <u>are quite</u>
<u>affectionate</u>., **16.** Florence returned to London and became
the supervisor of a hospital., **17.** England entered the war,
and Florence joined the War Office as a nurse.

page 67
1. Say—mild, **2.** Hooray—strong, **3.** Well—mild, **4.** Wow—
strong, **5.** Hey—strong, **6.–10.** Sentences will vary.
Suggested: **6.** Aha! That's the way to pitch., **7.** Oops! She
missed that one., **8.** Oh, she'll hit it next time., **9.** Hooray!
What a hit she made!, **10.** Wow! Look at her go!, Sentences
will vary.

page 68
1. sentence, **2.** sentence fragment, **3.** sentence, **4.** sentence
fragment, **5.** run-on sentence, **6.** sentence fragment,
7. sentence fragment, **8.** sentence, **9.** run-on sentence,
10. sentence fragment, **11.–13.** Sentences will vary.

page 69
Sentences will vary.

page 70
Paragraphs will vary. Suggested:
    I should begin by telling you how long I have been a
customer of Ronnie's. I have shopped at Ronnie's for five
years. I have always been satisfied with your merchandise
and your service.
    I am happy to have an opportunity to tell you how much
I have enjoyed shopping at Ronnie's. However, my letter
has a different purpose. I want to ask you to carry my
favorite line of sporting goods, Sporty's. I have begun
shopping elsewhere for sporting goods. I would rather be
shopping at Ronnie's because it is my favorite store.
Besides, your other customers would enjoy Sporty's top-
quality goods available at Ronnie's low prices.
    Please consider my suggestion. Let me know what you
decide.

page 71
1. clause, **2.** phrase, **3.** phrase, **4.** clause, **5.** phrase, **6.** clause,
7. phrase, **8.** phrase, **9.** clause, **10.** clause, **11.** clause,
12. phrase, **13.** clause, **14.–17.** Sentences will vary.

page 72
1. Cleopatra lived in ancient Egypt, <u>which she ruled</u>.; which,
2. She ruled with her brother <u>until he seized the throne</u>.; until,
3. She regained her throne <u>because Julius Caesar helped her</u>.;
because, **4.** Mark Antony ruled Rome <u>after Caesar died</u>.; after,
5. Antony went to Egypt, <u>where he lived for several years</u>.;
where, **6.** Antony and Cleopatra died <u>when a Roman army</u>
<u>attacked Egypt</u>.; when, **7.** <u>If you go to New York City</u>,
consider a visit to Brooklyn.; If, **8.** Fifteen teenagers there
gained some fame <u>because they were pollution fighters</u>.;

because, **9.** They chose the name Toxic Avengers, <u>which was</u>
<u>borrowed from a pollution-fighting superhero</u>.; which,
10. <u>Although it was located next to a school</u>, the Radiac
Research Corporation was storing large amounts of medical
waste.; Although, **11.** <u>When the Toxic Avengers heard about</u>
<u>this</u>, they planned a response.; When, **12.** <u>When a crowd</u>
<u>gathered for a public rally</u>, the teens told the people about
Radiac.; When, **13.** Public awareness grew <u>after the rally was</u>
<u>held</u>.; after

page 73
1. compound, **2.** complex, **3.** complex, **4.** compound,
5. complex, **6.** complex, **7.** compound, **8.** complex,
9. compound, **10.** complex

page 74
Answers and stories will vary.

page 75
1. Have you ever lost your voice?, **2.** What a strange feeling
that is!, **3.** You try to talk, but you can only squeak., **4.** No
one can understand you., **5.** The climbers left their base
camp at six in the morning., **6.** Mr. Enami is a train
engineer., **7.** Miles found his math problems to be very
challenging., **8.** Does the community softball league meet
every Friday?, **9.** Pedro and I go to the museum in
California., **10.** He is such a conscientious student!

page 76
Commas and semicolons should be placed after words
listed. **1.** runway, **2.** paper, cardboard, **3.** unloaded, sorted,
4. her, **5.** gear, **6.** Greek, Latin, **7.** Hey, **8.** agree, **9.** Noah,
Carrie, **10.** Dallas, Phoenix, **11.** worse; **12.** pilot, copilot,
13. Oh, **14.** captain; **15.** great, **16.** light,

page 77
Punctuation may vary. **1.** The city council just approved a
budget of $25 million—<u>up from $8 million only two years</u>
<u>ago</u>., **2.** Cecilia's best friend, <u>Marguerite</u>, found a stray
puppy in the park., **3.** Last week, Ms. Ten (<u>a local knitter</u>)
opened a yarn shop downtown., **4.** My mom, <u>a world-class</u>
<u>skier</u>, has a wall full of medals., **5.** The dachshund—<u>bred to</u>
<u>hunt badgers</u>—is known for its short legs and long body.,
6. Archie, <u>who just bought a kayak</u>, hopes to take it to the
lake this weekend., **7.** Maude, <u>on the other hand</u>, would
prefer to stay on the shore., **8.** Earlier this year, Magi (<u>my</u>
<u>friend from Alaska</u>) visited Russia., **9.** The Hope
diamond—<u>the most famous in the world</u>—is owned by the
Smithsonian., **10.** Mr. Blair, <u>who likes to play tennis</u>, also
likes to play golf., **11.** The study of animals—<u>also called</u>
<u>zoology</u>—is fascinating., **12.** Ocelots, <u>which are found in</u>
<u>South America</u>, are also called dwarf leopards.

page 78
1. Beth Ann Drake, **2.** President Lincoln, **3.** Central
Bookstore, **4.** Waco, Texas, **5.** Logan, Utah, **6.** Italian marble,

7. me, myself, and I, **8.** English accent, **9.** Union army, **10.** American citizen, **11.** Adams Middle School, **12.** Beauty and the Beast, **13.** Latin Club, **14.** Amelia Earhart Boulevard, **15.** Declaration of Independence, **16.** Yellowstone National Park, **17.** Mexican pottery, **18.** New Year's Day

page 79
1. lb, **2.** oz, **3.** ft, **4.** yd, **5.** ME, **6.** mg, **7.** L, **8.** cc, **9.** USPS, **10.** NBA, **11.** Rodeo Dr., **12.** Old Post Rd., **13.** Fifth Ave., **14.** NCAA, **15.** M.D., **16.** mph, **17.** rpm, **18.** F, **19.** C, **20.** Best Carpet Cleaners, Inc., **21.** The Farley Farragut Co., **22.** Dr. Thomas Gorman

page 80
Joe Bob's Restaurant: Answers will vary.
Student Information Card: School: The Parker School, Address: 120 Grant Ave., Ponca City, OK, Principal: Helena A. Ramírez, First day of school: Sept. 8, 2014, School day begins: 8:15 A.M., School day ends: 3:30 P.M.

page 81
1. Around the World in Eighty Days, **2.** The Pirates of Penzance, **3.** Profiles in Courage, **4.** Stalking the Wild Asparagus, **5.** The Cat Ate My Gymsuit, **6.** "Shake, Rattle, and Roll", **7.** "Twist and Shout", **8.** "Me and My Shadow", **9.** The Red Balloon, **10.** The Wizard of Oz, **11.** Stand by Me, **12.** "The Body", **13.** Cujo, Christine, Carrie, **14.** "Stand by Me", **15.** Time, **16.** Travels with Charley, **17.** "Welcome to Pittsburgh", **18.** Monday Night Football, **19.** Gorillas in the Mist

page 82
1. Leon dragged the huge crate through and shouted, "I'm home, Mom!", **2.** "She isn't back yet," Leon's brother told him., **3.** "Oh, Leon," said his brother, staring at the box, "what is that?", **4.** "Queen Elizabeth I ruled a great empire," Marcia said., **5.** She told her critics, "I have the heart and stomach of a king.", **6.** "Who else had a great impact on a country?" asked Terri., **7.** "Well," Ben remarked, "Mohandas Gandhi inspired a nonviolent revolution in India.", **8.** "Gandhi inspired Martin Luther King!" Terri added., **9.** "New York has a new program," Nancy said, "for student ticket buyers."

page 83
1. The **company**, High Flyers, forgot to include instructions., **2.** The **Eagle**, our only car, would not start., **3.** **Jim Delgado,** our next-door neighbor, came to help., **4.** Even **Jim**, a good mechanic, could not start it., **5.** The **starter**, an electric motor, was not working., **6.** The **pilot**, Captain Songrossi, said to fasten our seat belts., **7.** A **prairie**, a kind of grassland, is home to many kinds of plants and animals., **8.** Our **teacher**, Ms. Pesek, does not agree., **9.** Our favorite **store**, Video Visions, has many

unusual movies., **10.** My youngest **sister,** Sandra, asks to go there every Friday. **11.–12.** Sentences will vary.

page 84
1. I'd; I would, **2.** I've; I have, **3.** she's; she is, **4.** isn't; is not, **5.** We've; We have, **6.** They've; They have, **7.** I'm; I am, **8.** aren't; are not, **9.** didn't; did not, **10.** They'd; They would, **11.** wasn't; was not, **12.** haven't; have not, **13.** You've; You have, **14.** can't; cannot, **15.** Doesn't; Does not, **16.–20.** Sentences will vary. **16.** shouldn't, **17.** won't, **18.** he'd, **19.** let's, **20.** you're

page 85
1. extracurricular—beyond the curriculum, **2.** inactive—not active, **3.** impolite—not polite, **4.** prejudge—judge before, **5.** unusual—not usual, **6.** overconfident—having too much confidence, **7.** postelection—coming after an election

page 86
1. thoughtful; ful, **2.** grayish; ish, **3.** rainy; y, **4.** restless; less, **5.** harmful; ful, **6.–23.** Answers will vary. Suggested: artist, attendant, audiophile, boxer, capitalism, celebrant, contestant, criticism, cyclist, employment, government, humanoid, organizer, photograph, radiograph, skier, spheroid, thermometer

page 87
1. great-uncle, **2.** three-bedroom, **3.** mountain range, **4.** Everyone, **5.** cuckoo clock, **6.** sunset, **7.** seaweed, **8.** jellyfish, **9.** starfish, **10.** blue-green, **11.** sea lion, **12.** palm trees, **13.** fast-sinking, **14.** three-fourths, **15.** beachfront, **16.** spellbound, **17.** inner tube, **18.** newspaper, **19.** jack-of-all-trades, **20.** earring, **21.–24.** Answers will vary.

page 88
1. b, **2.** a, **3.** a, **4.** b, **5.** a, **6.** b, **7.** b, **8.** a, **9.** a, **10.** b

page 89
Definitions will vary. Suggestions are given. **1.** plenty of, **2.** exact, **3.** important, **4.** obstruction, **5.** large, **6.** isolated, **7.** work together, **8.** boring

page 90
Answers will vary. Suggested: **1.** sick, **2.** started, **3.** late, **4.** test, **5.** back, **6.** no one, **7.** left, **8.** quiet, **9.** left, **10.** finish, **11.** difficult, **12.** right, **13.–18.** Answers will vary. Suggested: **13.** untamed; tame, **14.** daring; timid, **15.** bulky; thin, **16.** lucky; unfortunate, **17.** fix; break, **18.** collect; scatter

page 91
1. gentle, **2.** pulled tight, **3.** a group of ships, **4.** cracked into pieces, **5.** air; heir, **6.** rode; road, **7.** thrown; throne, **8.** side; sighed

page 92
1. as busy as a bee; simile, **2.** sun smiled; personification, **3.** as cold as ice; simile, **4.** face was a mask; metaphor, **5.** I

Answer Key
Core Skills Language Arts, Grade 6

could eat a horse; hyperbole, **6.** as snug as a bug in a rug; simile, **7.** a thousand times; hyperbole, **8.** well-oiled machine; metaphor, **9.** as fast as a cheetah; simile, **10.** it touches the sky; hyperbole, **11.** forest fire; metaphor, **12.** I froze to death; hyperbole, **13.** rays of light danced; personification

page 93

Answers to analogies may vary; suggestions are given.
1. relative; item/category, **2.** car; part/whole, **3.** exhaustion; cause/effect, **4.** cat; part/whole, **5.** spice; item/category, **6.** grief; cause/effect, **7.** week; part/whole, **8.** cold; cause/ effect, **9.** library; part/whole, **10.** anxiety; cause/effect, **11.** dog; part/whole, **12.** fruit; item/category, **13.** dog; item/ category

page 94

1. antique, **2.** young, **3.** cozy, **4.** unhurried, **5.** simple, **6.** rare, **7.** Blackened, **8.** sip, **9.** tough, **10.** greasy, **11.** crumbly, **12.** soggy, **13.** loud, **14.** inferno

page 95

Dialogue will vary. Idioms: the cat got your tongue; hold your horses; knock your socks off; get off my back; on pins and needles; keep my nose to the grindstone; take off; get on the ball; about to burst; Lend me a hand

page 96

Answers will vary. Suggestions for tones: positive, formal, mysterious

page 97

1. first person; my, I, me, **2.** excited, but not expecting to be surprised, Continuations of story will vary., **3.–4.** Answers will vary.

page 98

Answers will vary.

page 99

Order of sentences: c, d, f, b, e, a, Transitions may vary, but suggestions are given: **1.** One morning, **2.** At first, **3.** Gradually, **4.** Initially, **5.** Suddenly, **6.** Instead

page 100

1.–6. Answers will vary.

page 101

Errors are corrected in bold type.

What an amazing experience my **brothers** and I had with the wind last **autumn**! We had driven with our parents to Point Reyes, north of San **Francisco**. Point Reyes is known as one of the **windiest** spots in the **country**, and on that day the winds were raging up to 50 miles an hour all along the California coast.

I had no way of determining the speed of the wind at Point **Reyes** that afternoon. I can only tell you that when we jumped into the air, we were blown a full five feet before landing**.**

The wind picked us up and carried us with the force of **rushing** water. **We simply** could not fall backward. The wind was so strong that we could lean back against it and let it support us as firmly as a brick wall would.

[paragraph ident] My brothers and I decided to take a short walk downwind along the beach. We allowed the wind to push us along at a **rapid** pace. For a while, we **stopped** walking altogether. We simply jumped into the air, let ourselves be blown along like empty milk **cartons**, and landed. Then, we jumped into the air again. Borne by the wind, we progressed as quickly as if we had been walking**.**
1. brothers, **2.** autumn, **3.** windiest, **4.** country, **5.** rushing, **6.** simply, **7.** rapid, **8.** stopped, **9.** cartons

pages 102–103

Graphic organizers and personal narratives will vary.

page 104

Topic sentence: The room had clearly been ransacked.,
1. Suggested answers: open and empty drawers, strewn clothes, empty closet, portrait of a solemn young woman— all sight; crunch of glass—hearing; fragrance of perfume, garlic smell—smell; broken glass underfoot—touch,
2. space order, **3.** Suggested answers: next to, trail . . . led, underfoot, on the wall

page 105

Errors are corrected in bold type.

A set of smooth stone steps **led** up to a flat clearing in the forest**.** Here, the sun's rays filtered down through the branches of the towering pines, and the ground was covered with **fragrant** green pine needles. **The** carpet of needles felt thick and soft under Nina's feet.

A gentle breeze rustled the branches**.** Nina inhaled the scent of the pines as it drifted on the breeze. **Mingled** with the scent of pine was the smell of the pale green **mosses** growing on the north sides of the trees.

[paragraph indent] What was that in the **middle** of the clearing? Nina saw a large stump, just under three **feet** tall and a full three feet in diameter. **Four** smaller stumps were **arranged** around it**.** Paul was already seated on one of the smaller stumps, and the large stump was clearly just the right **height** for a table.

On the large stump lay a basket of **juicy** blackberries, a canteen, and two shiny metal cups**.** Paul looked up at Nina and asked, "Are you ready for a treat?"
1. led, **2.** fragrant, **3.** mingled, **4.** mosses, **5.** middle, **6.** feet, **7.** arranged, **8.** height, **9.** juicy

pages 106–107

Graphic organizers and descriptive paragraphs will vary.

page 108

Sentences should be in this order: 3, 2, 4, 5, 7, 1, 6; Paragraphs will vary.

Answers may vary; suggestions are given: Before; First;
Then; When; Once; During. Steps will vary.

page 110
Answers will vary; suggestions are given. **French Onion Soup**: Cooking time: 40 minutes; Serves: 4; Ingredients: 2 onions, 1 cup shredded Swiss cheese, 28 ounces broth, 2 Tbsp butter, 2 garlic cloves, 4 slices of toast; 1. Chop the onions and place them in a saucepan with the butter. Cook on medium heat until onions are tender.; 2. Chop the garlic cloves and add them to the onions. Cook for 2 minutes, but don't let the garlic burn.; 3. Add the broth and bring to a boil.; 4. Take 4 bowls and sprinkle half of the shredded cheese into them.; 5. Carefully, pour the soup into the bowls.; 6. Lay a piece of toast over the top of each bowl of soup and sprinkle the rest of the cheese over the toast., **How to Pass a Math Test**: Passing a math test can be difficult if you do not understand the material being covered. When your teacher announces an upcoming test, ask if she can give you extra help after class or suggest different ways to study. Ask your friends if they'd like to study together. At home, create a quiet space so you can concentrate on the material. The night before the test, turn off the TV early so you can get enough sleep. Eat a good breakfast the morning of the test. Taking these steps will help you pass the test!

page 111
Errors are corrected in bold type.

With the help of a little tuna fish and some acting skill, you can easily get your dog Titan to take his pill. As you know, Titan often begs for **tuna,** but you never give him any. If you suddenly offer Titan some tuna with the pill inside it, he will become **suspicious** and refuse **to** eat it. Try this method instead.

Make a small ball of tuna **around** Titan's pill. Put the tuna ball on a plate. Then, find **something** you like to eat and put that on the plate, too. Take your plate and sit down at the kitchen table.

Titan will probably be watching you **carefully,** but you should ignore him. He's a very smart dog**,** and it will not be easy to **fool** him. **Your** chances of **success** are best if you [delete extra if] just pretend you don't see him.

[paragraph indent] Titan will soon sit **beside** you [delete comma] and start to beg. Eat your own food and continue to ignore Titan. Then, very **casually,** allow the ball of tuna to fall to the floor. You should make a quick grab for the tuna**,** but you must be sure that Titan gets to it first. Titan will eagerly gulp the tuna—and the pill.
1. tuna, 2. suspicious, 3. around, 4. something, 5. carefully,
6. fool, 7. success, 8. beside, 9. casually

pages 112–113
Graphic organizers and how-to paragraphs will vary.

page 114
1. circle: new house, old house; underline: similar to, Like, In addition, both, also, both, Furthermore, and so did; compare, 2. circle: new house, old house; underline: different, on the other hand, Unlike, However; contrast. Old House: old, hardwood floors, rugs, two-story; Both: three bedrooms, two bathrooms, fireplace in living room, separate dining room; New House: brand new, wall-to-wall carpet, one-story

page 115
Errors are corrected in bold type.

People sometimes **ask** me who my best **friend** is. Truthfully, I do not know. I have two close friends, and I like them both very much.

My friends **Judy** and Margie **are** alike in many ways. Both are **intelligent**, loyal, and helpful**.** Either can carry on a **great** conversation. Each has an **excellent** sense of humor, and we all enjoy many of the same activities.

However, my two friends are different in many ways. I **have** more **arguments** with Judy. She complains if she does not like something, and she **argues** if she disagrees with me. Margie **rarely** complains or argues, so we almost never **fight**.

On the other hand, Judy is a more honest friend. She always says exactly what she thinks or feels. In contrast, **Margie** never **says** anything negative to me about **things I** have said or done. Instead, she may say something to someone else, and her comments often **get** back to me. If Judy has a complaint, she **discusses** it with the person who has caused the problem.
1. friend, 2. intelligent, 3. great, 4. excellent, 5. arguments,
6. argues, 7. rarely, 8. things, 9. discusses

pages 116–117
Venn diagrams and compare and contrast paragraphs will vary.

page 118
1. emotional words, 2. testimonial, 3. bandwagon, 4. hasty generalization, 5.–6. Answers will vary.

page 119
1.–5. Answers will vary.

page 120
1.–5. Answers will vary.

page 121
Errors are corrected in bold type.

Zoos are an important to society and should receive more funding. **Zoos** provide scientists the **opportunity** to study and work with many different animals. With this knowledge, scientists can help preserve the lives of **endangered** species. Endangered species can be mated with subspecies so that they may be returned to the wild and removed from the endangered **list.** This has saved the **European** bison and the Hawaiian goose from becoming extinct. The **Manatee Rescue and Rehabilitation** Program is an example of how zoos help protect endangered **species.** This program cares for injured, sick, and orphaned **manatees** at different zoos and aquariums. When possible, the rehabilitated manatees are **released** back into the wild.

In addition, **zoos** also provide education for the public. Zoos have many different species of animals that are not native to the **United States. Animals** such as aardvarks, zebras, and **giant** pandas live in exhibits that are meant to be like their natural habitats. **Interactive** educational **exhibits** focus on saving the animals' habitats and educating **visitors** about the ways humans and wildlife can live together.

1. opportunity, **2.** endangered, **3.** species, **4.** manatees, **5.** released, **6.** exhibits, **7.** Interactive, **8.** Visitors

pages 122–123
Graphic organizers and persuasive essays will vary.

page 124
1. title page, **2.** foreword/preface, **3.** bibliography, **4.** copyright page, **5.** contents page

page 125
1. glossary, **2.** contents page, **3.** copyright page, **4.** title page, **5.** bibliography, **6.** title page, **7.** foreword/preface, **8.** contents page, **9.–15.** Responses will vary. Suggested: **9.** the date a book was published, **10.** title and author of book; publisher; where published, **11.** introductory comments about the book, **12.** list of all the topics in the book and the page numbers where they appear in the book, **13.** definitions of difficult or unfamiliar words that appear in the book, **14.** chapter titles; page numbers on which chapters begin, **15.** other books on the same topic

page 126
I. main topic, **A.** subtopic, **1.** detail, **2.** detail, **B.** subtopic, **1.** detail, **2.** detail, **3.** detail,
II. Killer Whales (Orcas)
    A. Interesting facts
       1. In dolphin family
       2. wide range of prey
    B. What it looks like
       1. Black bodies with white patches
       2. 26–28 feet long
Outlines will vary.

page 127
Notes should include key ideas. Suggested responses:
The Ring of Fire: a zone of active volcanoes around the rim of the Pacific Ocean; eight tectonic plates meet there; other volcanoes way from the rim sit over "hot spots."
Tsunamis: giant waves in the ocean that can travel far and at high speeds, up to 450 miles per hour; can be caused by earthquakes; the worst tsunami in history occurred in 2004 and killed over 200,000 people.

page 128
Answers will vary.

page 129
1. noun, **2.** two, **3.** Born in the area or country stated, **4.** nation, **5.** Born, grown, or living naturally in a particular area, **6.** nature, **7.** three, **8.** yes

page 130
1. almanac or encyclopedia, **2.** thesaurus, **3.** encyclopedia, **4.** dictionary, **5.** *Books in Print*

Answer Key
Core Skills Language Arts, Grade 6

4500782362
September 4, 2019
Printed in the U.S.A